Chinese GCSE

中学汉语
Student's Book Vol.3

主 编 李晓琪 **副主编** 罗青松
编 者 宣 雅 王淑红 刘晓雨

华语教学出版社·伦敦
Sinolingua · London

Every effort has been made to trace all copyright holders, but if any have been inadvertently overlooked, the publishers will be pleased to make the necessary arrangements at the first opportunity.

Chinese GCSE (Student's Book Vol.3)

Compiler-in-chief: Xiaoqi LI
Deputy compiler-in-chief: Qingsong LUO
Compilers: Ya XUAN, Shuhong WANG, Xiaoyu LIU

Adviser: Xiaoming ZHANG
Consultant editors: Hongxia DU, Jingjing ZHAO, Lu LIN

Editors: Shurong ZHAI, Ranran DU
Cover design: Gu Shou
Layout/Illustration: 清鑫工作室
QING XING Studio

Copyright ©2014 by Sinolingua London Ltd.
First published in Great Britain in July 2014 by **Sinolingua London Ltd.**
Unit 13, Park Royal Metro Centre
Britannia Way
London NW10 7PA
Tel: +44(0)2089519305
Email: editor@sinolingualondon.com
Website: www.sinolingua.com.cn

Printed in China

ISBN 978-1-907838-06-4

编写说明

　　《中学汉语》是为以英语为母语的11-16岁中学生编写的汉语教材，全套教材分为三个等级（第一册、第二册和第三册）九本书，每个等级包括学生用书（课本）、教师用书和练习册。全套教材还配有字词卡片、挂图以及CD-ROM、PPT课件等多媒体产品。每册教材可使用一学年（参考学时为90-100学时），全套教材可以供三个年级使用。

一、设计框架

　　《中学汉语》采用了以新版GCSE大纲交际话题为主线，以语言项目为核心，以文化内容为基本要素的综合性构架，力求做到设计理念与时俱进，语言知识扎实科学，文化内涵丰富生动。

1. 以话题为主线

　　教材每册有八个单元，每个单元由相关话题的三篇课文组成。每册教材都基本涵盖了Edexcel新版GCSE、AQA中文大纲的主要话题的相关内容，并参照了Asset Language的语言学习要求。教材围绕话题主线，针对不同等级，在语言形式、文化内容上逐步拓展丰富。这种编排方式使学习者无论选取任何阶段的教材，都可较全面地接触新版GCSE大纲的交际话题，从而在提高交际能力，以及准备考试方面得到帮助。如：初学者可以在学完第一、二册后，参加GCSE考试，第三册则用于巩固提高，并逐步向AS过渡。而具备一定汉语基础的学生，也可以直接从第二册或第三册开始学习。

2. 以语言项目为核心

　　教材以新版GCSE大纲提供的560个核心词语和85个语法项目为教材内容的重点与核心，全套教材覆盖了新大纲的全部语言项目——词汇和语言点。此外，还根据日常交际需要，以及教学对象、学习环境的特点，进行了合理调整与拓展，以达到在控制教材难度的基础上，丰富教材内容，满足话题表达需求的目的。教材各等级语言项目分布如下：

　　　　第一册：汉字145个左右，生词237个，句型91个。
　　　　第二册：汉字150个左右，生词233个，句型93个。
　　　　第三册：汉字160个左右，生词230个，句型95个。

　　书中句型除了在新版大纲基础上进行拓展之外，编写组还从教材语言点设置与编排的科学性与实用性出发，将新版大纲中概括表述的句型具体化，并进行合理分级。如在新版GCSE中文大纲中，情态动词只作为一个语言点给出，用"他会说普通话"概括这一语言形式，我们在教材中处理为"他能说普通话"、"你应该学习中文"等多个语言点。这样不仅更全面地表现出情态动词的特点，也便于在教学中分解难点，科学、合理、有序、全面地安排教学内容。

3. 以文化内容为基本要素

　　《中学汉语》注重文化内容，并将其与语言学习目标、教学对象与教学环境结合起来加以体现。本套教材的文化内容反映在话题设计、课文内容、练习设计、画面展示、教学提示等方面，以期逐步培养学习者的目的文化意识，拓展他们的文化视野；而通过教材丰富多样的文化体现，也可进一步增强教材的知识性与趣味性。

二、教材结构

1. 学生用书

学生用书是教材的核心。每课的基本版块有学习目标提示、课文、词语以及听说读写译练习。学生用书上的练习作为课堂操练使用，主要围绕教学目标，从听说读写译几个方面进行操练。每三课为一个单元，每个单元后有句型小结，帮助学生总结语言知识；同时，还设置了与单元话题相关的文化，以增进学生对中国文化的感性认识。学生用书的编写原则是简明、适用，符合课堂教学需要，同时又注重效果，循序渐进地增进学生的语言技能与文化认知。

2. 教师用书

教师用书的主要作用是帮助教师较为便捷地在内容、方法上进行教学准备。每课的基本版块有：教学内容提示、教学步骤与建议、练习参考答案、相关语言知识点和文化背景知识的简要说明，此外，还根据教学需要，提供了一些课堂活动和小游戏。每个单元提供了一套单元测验题，考题设计综合了单元学习内容，形式上也逐步靠近GCSE考试题型。教师在教学中可用于考查学生阶段学习情况，从而循序渐进地帮助学生适应考试，最终达到GCSE考试的标准。

3. 练习册

练习册为教材提供外围的辅助练习，练习安排与学生用书中的练习相辅相成，作为课堂练习的拓展，供学习者课下使用，或用来丰富课堂训练项目。提供多样化的练习，可以进一步充实课堂教学的内容；提供有选择的练习，也可以让学生有机会自主学习，增强自学能力。

4. 其他配套资源

为方便使用者，本套教材还有生词卡片、多媒体材料等，增加教与学的互动性和生动性，方便师生课堂教学和自学。

三、教材特色

《中学汉语》关注教学对象的特点，注重使用者的基本目的和要求，教材的突出特点表现为以下几个方面。

1. 针对性与目的性统一

本套教材针对中学阶段的英语为母语的汉语学习者编写。通过本套教材的学习，学生可全面提高汉语交际能力，并在听说读写技能上全面达到GCSE中文考试大纲的标准和要求。

2. 全面性与基础性统一

本套教材在话题、语音、汉字、词汇、句型、文化等方面，全面覆盖新版GCSE中文考试大纲的内容；同时，根据学生水平等级、交际需要及汉语本身的特点进行全面规划，合理增补，科学编排。同时，教材设计也充分考虑到中学生汉语学习的基本目标与认知特点，突出基础知识、基本技能的掌握，注重内容编排难度、容量、梯级的合理性。

3．科学性与趣味性统一

教材针对教学对象的特点，体现寓教于乐的编写理念。话题贴近学生现实生活，生活场景的设置真实自然，课文内容自然活泼，练习形式丰富多样，注重实用性和互动性。此外，教材还通过图文并茂的文化介绍，拓展学生文化视野，增强教材的趣味性，从而使得学习者获得有趣、有用的汉语学习体验。

为此套教材的策划和出版，华语教学出版社的王君校社长、韩晖总编和伦敦分社的茹静总经理，以及责任编辑翟淑蓉、杜然然付出了大量的心血，对此我们表示衷心的感谢；此外英国的张小明、杜宏霞、赵晶晶、林璐四位老师和梁乔、何晓红、吴允红、黄珍理等诸位一线教师的积极参与，为本教材的问世给予了很大的帮助，我们编写组的全体成员对你们也说一声：谢谢！

设计一套全面系统的针对性教材，是一项有挑战性的工作，需要长期努力。我们的错误和疏漏在所难免，期望各位同仁提出宝贵意见，我们将不断完善，使《中学汉语》更好地为课堂教学提供帮助。

《中学汉语》编写组

Compilers' Words

Chinese GCSE is designed for secondary school students in English speaking countries who are aged between 11 and 16. This three-volume series covers three levels. Each level includes a student's book, a workbook, a teacher's book, Chinese character flash cards, wall charts, and multimedia support through CD-ROMs and PowerPoint courseware. Each volume corresponds to one academic year (90-100 class hours) and the whole series can be used consecutively over three grades.

Design Framework

Chinese GCSE is organized according to the new GCSE syllabus with a topic-oriented structure that takes the language as its core and the cultural content as its key element. The series is thus designed as a full set of materials, which includes both comprehensive language knowledge and enriched cultural content.

1. Key Topics

The series covers all the areas in the new Edexcel Chinese GCSE and AQA syllabis, and takes the Asset Language requirements as its reference. Each volume has eight units, with each unit containing three lessons that focus on one topic or activity. The vocabulary and grammar develop step by step so that students can familiarise themselves with new topics covered by the Chinese GCSE, while simultaneously developing their conversational skills as they prepare for the exam. Beginners may take the GCSE exam after completing the first two volumes, and then take the third volume as a preparatory guide for the AS exam. Those who have a certain command of the Chinese language may start from either volume 2 or 3.

2. Language as the Core

The series covers all the 560 core words and 85 grammar points required by the new Chinese GCSE syllabus. On top of this, the contents have been organized and extended to satisfy the daily communicative needs of the learners, while also ensuring the inclusion of extensive extra content and expressions, all of which are based on the Chinese GCSE course requirements. The language points are arranged as follows: .

> Volume 1: 145 Chinese characters, 237 new words, 91 sentence patterns
>
> Volume 2: 150 Chinese characters, 233 new words, 93 sentence patterns
>
> Volume 3: 160 Chinese characters, 230 new words, 95 sentence patterns

The sentence patterns have been extended based on the new Chinese GCSE syllabus, and have been substantiated and sequenced according to their level of difficulty. For example, in the new Chinese GCSE syllabus, the modal verb is given as a language point and expressed in the sentence 他会说普通话. However, in this series we have modified that entry into several language points, such as 他能说普通话,你应该学习中文, etc. This more fully displays the characteristics of modal verbs, helps to ease learning difficulties, and provides a better organization and format of instruction.

3. Cultural Contents as the Key Elements

Chinese GCSE places an emphasis on cultural information, which is combined with language objectives and methods of teaching to provide a nurturing learning environment. As shown in the topics, texts, exercises, pictures and teaching tips of the series, the cultural contents are aimed at cultivating students' cultural consciousness and extending their cultural vision. This diversified cultural content renders the books more interesting and informative to students, which in turn makes them a more effective learning tool.

Structure of the Series

1. Student's Book

The Student's Book is the core book of the series. Each lesson consists of sections such as learning objectives, text, new words, and exercises for listening, speaking, reading, writing and translating which can be used as practical exercises in class. Three lessons form a unit, followed by a unit summary which reviews the language points of the lessons, and also includes cultural tips for a more comprehensive understanding of Chinese. The Student's Book is both concise and practical, and aims to develop the language learning skills and cultural recognition of the students in a gradual manner.

2. Teacher's Book

The Teacher's Book pedagogically prepares the instructors to teach the series' contents in a fun and nurturing learning environment. Each lesson includes teaching suggestions, keys to the exercises, and additional cultural information. Furthermore, it provides a number of suggestions for classroom activities and games. A test is provided after each unit based on its content, and is close to the GCSE test in format. This test can serve as a tool to gauge the students' progress, and further prepare them for the GCSE exams.

3. Workbook

This includes exercises as a complement to the Student's Book. As an extension of classroom exercises, it may be used both in class and at home. These exercises not only supplement classroom teaching, but also provide materials for self study and a chance for the students to improve their language abilities outside of class.

4. Additional Resources

The series also provides flash cards, and multimedia materials to increase the convenience of teaching and self study, making both the teaching and studying of this series a more interactive and dynamic process.

Features

This series has been closely tailored to meet students' basic objectives and studying needs. This has been done through the following:

1. Having an Aligned Focus

The target readers of the series are secondary school Chinese language students whose native language is English. Through their study, students can fully improve their communicative ability in Chinese, and reach the standard required to successfully sit the Chinese GCSE exam in listening, speaking, and reading and writing skills.

2. Fully Integrating Basic Language Knowledge

This series covers all the requirements of the new Chinese GCSE syllabus in its topics, phonetics, characters, vocabularies, sentences, cultural knowledge, etc. It is clearly organized into different levels of language ability and knowledge, social settings and characteristics of the Chinese language. The objectives and recognition patterns of secondary school students have been fully taken into consideration. It emphasizes cementing a solid command, as well as introducing students to more difficult and advanced language points to encourage further study.

3. Being Practical and Fun to Use

The topics covered relate to the students' real lives, and include realistic scenarios; the content is dynamic, and the exercises are diverse, practical and useful. Through illustrated cultural introductions, this series hopes to expand the cultural visions of the students, and as a result of this, we hope the students will in turn have a rewarding experience learning Chinese.

For their help and support during the compilation of this series, we would like to extend our heartfelt thanks to Mr. Wang Junxiao, President of Sinolingua, Ms. Han Hui, Editor-in-chief of Sinolingua, Ms. Ru Jing, Managing Director of Sinolingua London Ltd., as well as Sinolingua editors Zhai Shurong and Du Ranran. Thanks also go to Zhang Xiaoming, Du Hongxia, Zhao Jingjing, Lin Lu and many other teachers in Britain.

It's a challenge to compile a series of textbooks that is both comprehensive and practical, and has clear academic focus. We have thoroughly enjoyed this process of creation and we welcome the opinions and comments of our peers and students alike.

Characters in the Text

大海 中国人
Dàhǎi

小雨 中国人
Xiǎoyǔ

天天 中国人
Tiāntiān

京京 中国人
Jīngjīng

Characters in the Text

大卫 David 英国人
Dàwèi

玛丽 Mary 英国人
Mǎlì

本 Ben 英国人
Běn

丽丽 Lily 英国人
Lìli

职业
zhíyè
Vocation

教师	医生	记者	音乐家
jiàoshī	yīshēng	jìzhě	yīnyuèjiā
teacher	doctor	reporter	musician

工程师	画家	导游	店员
gōngchéngshī	huàjiā	dǎoyóu	diànyuán
engineer	painter	tour guide	sales clerk

工人	销售人员	设计师	演员
gōngrén	xiāoshòu rényuán	shèjìshī	yǎnyuán
worker	salesperson	designer	actor/actress

方向
fāngxiàng
Direction

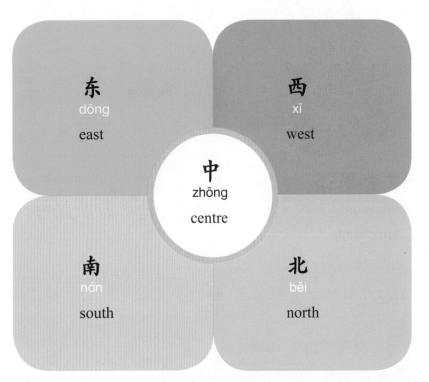

东
dōng
east

西
xī
west

中
zhōng
centre

南
nán
south

北
běi
north

社交用语
Social Greetings

Hello.	你好。
Hello, everyone.	大家好。
Good evening.	晚上好。
Good night.	晚安。
Goodbye.	再见。
See you tomorrow.	明天见。
Excuse me.	请问。
Thank you.	谢谢。
Sorry.	对不起。
It doesn't matter.	没关系。

课堂用语
Classroom Expressions

Good morning.	早上好。
Hello, Miss/Sir.	老师好。
Hello, everyone.	同学们好。
It's time for class.	现在上课。
Read after me.	跟我读。
Once again, please.	再说一遍。
Time for break.	休息一会儿。
Class is over.	现在下课。

目 录
CONTENTS

第一课 Lesson **1**

This Is My Business Card
这是我的名片

Learning Objectives

交际话题 Topic of conversation:
联系信息 Contact Information
Liánxì xìnxī

基本句型 Sentence patterns:
你是不是英国人？
名片上有我的地址和电话。
欢迎你来我们学校。

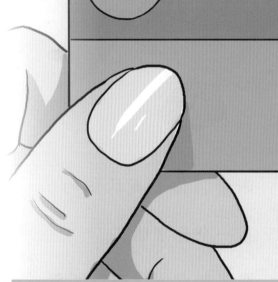

王大明
汉语老师

Address: 北京市海淀区花园路59号
Phone: 76219977
Email: xinpengyou@sina.com

New Words

1. 名片 míngpiàn　**n.** name card; (business) card
2. 可以 kěyǐ　**aux.** can, may
3. 联系 liánxì　**v.** to get in touch with; to contact
4. 外国 wàiguó　**n.** foreign country
5. 来自 láizì　**v.** to come from
6. 如果 rúguǒ　**conj.** if; in case
7. 这些 zhèxiē　**pron.** these
8. 交流 jiāoliú　**v.** to exchange
9. 话题 huàtí　**n.** topic, subject (of a talk or conversation)
10. 网址 wǎngzhǐ　**n.** website, (Internet) site
11. 网页 wǎngyè　**n.** web page
12. 路 lù　**n.** road, path, way
13. 不同 bù tóng　**adj.** different

Text

Part I

（飞机上，大卫和大明坐在一起。）

大明：你好。你也去北京？是去
　　　旅行吗？

大卫：我不是去旅行，我去北京
　　　学习。

大明：你是不是英国人？

大卫：是，我家在伦敦。你呢？

大明：我是北京人，我家在北京。
　　　你去过北京吗？

大卫：没有，这是我第一次去。
　　　你叫什么名字？

大明：我叫王大明，这是我的名片。
　　　míngpiàn
　　　到北京以后，你可以跟我联系。
　　　　　　　　　kěyǐ　　liánxì

大卫：谢谢你，大明。我叫大卫，
　　　认识你很高兴。

大明：名片上有我的地址和电话，
　　　你可以来找我，可以给我
　　　打电话。

大卫：谢谢。你是我认识的
　　　第一个北京朋友。

大明：我还可以给你介绍很多
　　　朋友。

大卫：太好了。到了北京我一定去
　　　找你。

大明：好的。欢迎你到北京。

欢迎你来周末学校

你想认识中国朋友吗？你想跟中国朋友一起说汉语吗？你想跟他们一起聊天儿、学习中国文化吗？如果你对这些活动感兴趣，欢迎你来周末学校。
zhèxiē

你想认识外国朋友吗？你想跟外国朋友一起说外语吗？你想学习他们
wàiguó
国家的文化吗？如果你有兴趣，欢迎你来我们学校。
rúguǒ

我们学校的学生来自很多国家，有中国人、英国人、法国人，还有美国
láizì
人、南非人；有亚洲的，也有欧洲的、美洲的和非洲的，他们希望认识新朋
Nánfēirén
友。我们的老师也都来自不同的国家。
bù tóng

周末，你在这里学习外语和文化，还可以认识新朋友，跟他们一起聊天儿。如果你周末没有时间来，你还可以在网络上跟这些朋友聊天儿，

交流你们喜欢的话题。
jiāoliú   huàtí

我们学校的网址是www.pengyou.com，网页上有学校课程和活动的介
wǎngzhǐ   wǎngyè
绍。如果你有兴趣，请联系我们。

电话：76219977

地址：北京市海淀区花园路59号
　　　　　hǎidiànqū　　lù

电子邮件：xinpengyou@sina.com

Exercises

Read 1 Put a cross in the correct box according to Part I of the Text.

1) Why does David go to Beijing?

A	B	C
To travel	To study	To go back home

2) What does Daming give to David?

A	B	C
His address	His phone	His business card

3) What will Daming probably do later with David?

A	B	C
Go to London to see David	Go to see David in Beijing	Introduce David to someone

Listen 2 Sam is telling about his after school programme. Listen to his story and answer the following questions in English.

1) What kind of activity did Sam have last week?

....

2) What were the other people there?

....

3) Who is Paul?

....

4) What does Daming do in Beijing now?

....

5) What did Daming tell Sam?

....

Read 3

Put a cross to the five correct answers according to Part II of the Text.

A If you want to chat with Chinese friends you can come to our school.

B If you want to teach foreign language you can come to our school.

C You can meet friends from different countries here.

D Our teachers are all from Europe.

E You can come to our school on weekends.

F You can chat with these friends on the Internet on weekends only.

G You can find information about courses and activities on our website.

H You can contact us if you have any questions.

Talk 4

Read the following paragraph and answer the questions below in Chinese.

　　半年前，朋友告诉我一个网址，那是一个网上学校。我在网页上看到他们有什么课程和活动，我对他们的课程和活动很感兴趣，就跟他们联系了。在这里我认识了几个新朋友，他们来自英国、法国和中国，还有一个来自非洲。有的时候我们在网上聊天儿，我们交流的话题很多，他们给我介绍他们的国家、城市和文化，我告诉他们我的学校、我的家人。他们都说，如果我以后去他们的国家、他们的城市，我要跟他们联系。我也希望他们能来英国。

1) How did 'I' know about this online school?

....

2) How can 'I' join those courses or activities?

....

3) Where are 'my' new friends from?

....

4) What do 'we' usually talk about?

....

Talk 5

You are going to talk about a new friend you've met. You will talk about:

1) How you met.

2) His/Her general information.

3) How you keep in touch with him/her.

4) What you usually talk about.

5) What you think about him/her.

Write 6

Essay Plan Form

Essay title:

A short passage for a local newspaper to introduce your school.

1) Name of your school

2) The students

3) The teachers

4) Courses and activities

5) What you think about your school

6) Contact information of your school

7) Invite readers to visit your school's website

Your conclusion

Read 7 Reorganize the following sentences and create a short paragraph.

1）欢迎你来周末学校。

2）我们学校的学生来自很多国家,有中国人、英国人、法国人,还有美国人、南非人。

3）在这里你可以认识新朋友,跟他们一起聊天儿,一起学习他们的文化。

4）你可以在学校的网页上看到课程和活动的介绍。

5）我们的网址是www.pengyou.com,电话:76219977,地址:北京市海淀区花园路59号。

6）我们的老师也都来自不同的国家。

第二课 Lesson 2

Come and Have a Try 你来试试吧！

Learning Objectives

交际话题 Topic of conversation:

介绍自己 Introducing Yourself
Jièshào zìjǐ

基本句型 Sentence patterns:

我除了英语以外，还会一点儿日语。
课程虽然不多，但是有点儿难。
你说得很好。
你来试试吧。

面试

New Words

1. 出生 chūshēng v. to be born
2. 日期 rìqī n. date
3. 年 nián n. year
4. 日语 Rìyǔ n. Japanese
5. 虽然 suīrán conj. although; even though
6. 但是 dànshì conj. but, yet, however,
7. 试试 shìshi v. to try, to test
8. 导游 dǎoyóu n. tour guide
9. 别的 biéde pron. other
10. 努力 nǔlì adv. hard
11. 赚钱 zhuàn qián v. to make money; to make a profit
12. 满意 mǎnyì adj. satisfied, pleased

Text

Part I

（大海走进了经理的办公室）

大海：　王经理，您好。我叫张大海，

　　　　我想做兼职，这是我的简历。

王经理：欢迎。你在报纸上看了广告，

　　　　是吗？

大海：　是的。我觉得这个工作很有意思。

王经理：你今年多大了？你的 出 生
　　　　　　　　　　　　　　chūshēng

　　　　日期是……
　　　　rìqī

大海：　我1997年8月21日出生，今年
　　　　　　　nián

　　　　16岁了。

王经理：你的外语怎么样？

大海：　我除了英语以外，还会一点儿

　　　　日语。
　　　　Rìyǔ

王经理：你可以用日语介绍你自己吗？

大海：　可以……

王经理：你说得很好。你以前做过兼职吗？

大海：　做过。我在学校图书馆工作过，

　　　　还做过学校报纸的兼职小记者。

王经理：很好。请问你这学期的课

　　　　程多吗？难不难？

大海：　课程虽然不多，但是有
　　　　　　suīrán　　　dànshì

　　　　点儿难。

王经理：那你还有时间兼职吗？

大海：　我会努力做好的。我一
　　　　　　nǔlì

　　　　边学习，一边做兼职。

王经理：好吧，你来试试吧！
　　　　　　　　　shìshi

大海：　谢谢！

Part II

我想做导游
dǎoyóu

我在报纸上看到旅行社找兼职导游的广告，我对汉语导游工作很感兴趣，想申请做这个工作。虽然我没做过导游，但是我有别的工作经验。我以
biéde
前教过法语、做过兼职记者，还在超市和学校图书馆工作过。做这些工作的时候，我都很努力。现在我还在学校学习汉语。我有很多中国朋友，我常常跟他们说汉语。我的汉语说得很好，我也喜欢写汉字、看中文杂志和报纸。放假的时候我常常去旅行，去过很多有意思的地方，有很多旅行经验。

我觉得学生做兼职很好，除了可以赚钱以外，还可以有工作经验，这
zhuàn qián
对将来找工作很有帮助。我希望可以到这个公司来试试，我一定努力工作。

我的校长给我写了介绍信，他介绍了我的学习成绩。他对我很满意，
xiàozhǎng   mǎnyì
还说学生做兼职很好，希望我能得到这个工作。

Exercises

Read
1
Put a cross in the correct box according to Part I of the Text.

1) What foreign language(s) can Dahai speak?

A	B	C
English	French	English and Japanese

2) What kind of part-time job(s) has Dahai had before?

A	B	C
Working at an advertising company	Working at school library	Teaching French

3) What does Dahai think of his courses at school?

A	B	C
Too many	Not very difficult	Difficult

Listen 2 You are listening to a boy's self-introduction. Answer the following questions in English.

1) What kind of part-time job has he got?

....

2) What does he think of his part-time job?

....

3) What do the others think of his work?

....

4) What does he want to do now?

....

5) What is he asking of the listeners?

....

Read 3 Put a cross to the five correct answers according to Part II of the text.

A He has read a part-time job advertisement on a website.

B He is interested in applying for the Chinese language tour guide.

C He has working experience as a tour guide.

D He is learning Chinese and he speaks Chinese very well.

E He travels a lot during his holidays.

F He doesn't think a part-time job will make him any money.

G He thinks that a part-time job is helpful for future job hunting.

H His principal has written him a letter of recommendation.

Read 4 Read the following paragraph and answer the questions below in Chinese.

王经理：

您好！

我是英伦学校的学生，我叫Tom，来自伦敦。我在今天的报纸上看到，您的公司有兼职工作，你们希望找会说汉语的英国人。我是英国人，出生在伦敦，我从2010年开始学习汉语。除了在学校学习，我还跟我的中国朋友学习，所以我学得很快。虽然我的汉字写得不太漂亮，但是我说汉语说得很好。我以前做过兼职工作，当过中文导游、服务员，他们对我都很满意。我希望可以到您的公司兼职工作。请您看看我的简历，希望我可以去试试。

Tom

1) Where does Tom come from?

....

2) What kind of person is this company looking for?

....

3) Where did Tom learn Chinese?

....

4) How is Tom's Chinese?

....

5) What kind of part-time job had Tom had before?

....

Talk 5 You are going to introduce Harry. You will talk about:

1) Harry's date of birth.

2) His foreign language proficiency.

3) His part-time working experience.

4) His teacher's letter of recommendation.

5) His contact information.

Write 6

Essay Plan Form

Essay title:
A job application letter.

1) Where you've heard of the information

2) The job you're applying for

3) Your personal information. For example, date of birth

4) What you're good at

5) Your working experience

6) Your employer's comments

Your conclusion

Read 7

Reorganize the following sentences and create a short paragraph.

1）虽然我没当过导游，但是我有别的工作经验。

2）我还去过很多地方，有很多旅游经验。

3）我以前教过法语、当过兼职记者，还在超市和学校图书馆工作过。

4）我希望可以到这个公司来试试，我一定努力工作。

5）做这些工作的时候，我都很努力。

6）我在报纸上看到旅行社找兼职导游的广告，我想申请做这个工作。

第三课 Lesson

3

I Think She Is the Right Person to Do This Job
我觉得她做这个工作很合适

Learning Objectives

交际话题 Topic of conversation:

推荐朋友 Recommending
Tuījiàn péngyou Your Friends

基本句型 Sentence patterns:

大学毕业以后，他就进了工厂。

他的理想是做一名记者。

他一有空就去旅行。

New Words

1 名 míng **m.w.** (a measure word used for persons)

2 大学 dàxué **n.** university

3 毕业 bìyè **v./n.** to graduate; graduation

4 工厂 gōngchǎng **n.** factory

5 聪明 cōngming **adj.** clever, intelligent

6 文章 wénzhāng **n.** writing, article

7 拍 pāi **v.** to take (a picture, photograph)

8 照片 zhàopiàn **n.** photograph, picture

9 份 fèn **m.w.** (a measure word used for papers)

10 笑 xiào **v.** to smile, to laugh

11 可爱 kě'ài **adj.** lovely, lovable

12 普通话 Pǔtōnghuà **n.** Putonghua; Mandarin Chinese

13 合适 héshì **adj.** suitable, appropriate

Text

Part I

大卫：京京，我们想找一个兼职记者，你有兴趣吗？

京京：对不起，这学期我的课太多了。除了在学校上课，我还在周末学校学习，我没有时间。

大卫：你能不能介绍一个朋友？

京京：小王可以吗？他的理想是做一名记者。
名 míng

大卫：他的外语怎么样？

京京：他除了会说汉语、英语以外，法语也说得很好。他很聪明，还喜欢写文章。
聪明 cōngming
文章 wénzhāng

大卫：他做过记者吗？

京京：没有。大学毕业以后，他就进了工厂。
毕业 bìyè
工厂 gōngchǎng

大卫：我们希望这个记者对旅行也感兴趣。

京京：小王特别喜欢旅游，他一有空就去旅行。他已经去过很多地方了，还拍了很多漂亮的照片。
拍 pāi
照片 zhàopiàn

大卫：希望小王对这个工作有兴趣。你可以问问他吗？

京京：好的。我一回家就给他打电话。

大卫：如果他有兴趣，请他准备一份简历。
份 fèn

京京：好。我一定告诉他。

她的普通话说得特别好
Pǔtōnghuà

中国学生要来我们学校，校长要找一个学生用汉语介绍我们的学校。

丽丽是我的朋友，比我大一岁。她很喜欢笑，每个看到她的人都
xiào
说她很可爱。因为她的爸爸妈妈去中国的工厂工作，所以，她就去了
kě'ài
中国，在中国的学校上学。

她在中国的时候，我们常常写电子邮件。有空的时候，我们也在
网上聊天儿。去年她小学毕业以后，回到英国上中学。她的普通话说
pǔtōnghuà
得特别好，她还知道很多中国故事，还会唱很多中国歌。丽丽很聪
明，跟她聊天儿很有趣，同学们都喜欢和她一起玩儿。每个星期五
放学以后，我们就去她家，和她一起做游戏。有的时候她也教我们
汉语，她还给我们介绍了几个中国朋友。我觉得她介绍我们的学校
很合适。
héshì

Exercises

Read 1 Put a cross in the correct box according to Part I of the Text.

1) What does Jingjing do besides going to school?

A	B	C
Work as a part-time journalist	Study at a weekend school	Work at a factory

2) What is Xiao Wang's ideal activity?

A	B	C
Be a journalist	Travel	Study a foreign language

3) What did Xiao Wang do after he graduated from middle school?

A	B	C
Became a journalist	Went to travel	Worked in a factory

Listen 2 You are listening to Jingjing's introduction of her friend. Answer the following questions in English.

1) What does Sam want to do this holiday?

....

2) What does Sam's father want him to do?

....

3) What does Sam like?

....

4) What does Sam usually do when he travels?

....

5) What is Sam's new job?

....

Read 3 Put a cross to the five correct answers according to Part II of the text.

A There are Chinese students coming to my school.

B I'm one year older than Lily.

C Lily likes to smile.

D Lily went to China to study in a primary school.

E Lily speaks Mandarin very well.

F Lily came back from China this year.

G I've introduced some Chinese friends to Lily.

H Lily has working experience.

Talk 4 Read the following paragraph and answer the questions below in Chinese.

　　张老师，我看了您的电子邮件，知道您要找一位英语教师。我有一个英国朋友，他很合适做这个工作。他叫Henry，也在周末中文学校学习汉语。他大学毕业以后，就去了中国。他非常聪明，以前没学过汉语，在周末中文学校学了一年时间，现在他的普通话比很多同学好。除了英语、汉语以外，他还会说法语和德语，我们都说他是外语天才（tiāncái, genius）。他也很可爱，很喜欢笑，知道很多有意思的故事，您的学生一定会喜欢他。

1) What does Mr. Zhang want?

....
2) Where did 'I' meet Henry?

....
3) When did Henry come to China?

....
4) Why do 'we' say Henry is a language genius?

....
5) Why do 'I' think Mr. Zhang's students are going to like Henry?

....

Talk
5

You are going to recommend a friend to work as a tour guide. You will talk about:

1）His name and age.

2）His Chinese proficiency.

3）His English proficiency.

4）His hobby.

5）His working experience.

6）Your conclusion.

Write
6

Essay Plan Form

Essay title:
Introduce a friend of you.

1) Where you've met him/her

2) Your general thought on him/her

3) Why you feel this way

4) His/Her hobbies

5) His/Her special experiences

6) What you usually do together with him/her

Your conclusion

Read 7 Reorganize the following sentences and create a short paragraph.

1）丽丽很聪明，也很可爱。

2）我的朋友丽丽申请了这个工作。

3）她在中国学校上过学，她的普通话说得非常好。

4）我觉得让她介绍我们的学校很合适。

5）她还知道很多中国故事，会唱很多中国歌。

6）中国学生要来我们学校，校长要找一个学生用汉语介绍我们的学校。

中国画

　　中国画又叫国画，它是用毛笔、墨及颜料，在宣纸或绢上画出的画。中国画从题材上分，主要有人物画、花鸟画和山水画。中国画构图灵活，可以同时表现不同时空的丰富多彩的自然景物，画家往往通过景物的描绘表达自己的感情，以及对自然与社会的认识。

Traditional Chinese Painting

Traditional Chinese painting is the art of painting on xuan paper (Chinese traditional rice paper) or silk, with a brush dipped in black or coloured ink. Figure paintings, bird-and-flower paintings, and landscape paintings are the most commonly-seen themes. It is rich in form and unique in style. Painters express their feelings and acknowledgment of the natural world and society through this style of painting.

第一单元小结 Unit One Summary	
1　某人＋可以＋介词词组。 Sb. + 可以 + preposition phrase.	你可以跟我联系。 You can contact me. 他可以给我打电话。 He can give me a ring.
2　欢迎＋某人＋动词词组。 欢迎 + sb. + verb phrase.	欢迎你来我们公司。 Welcome to our company. 欢迎他们去我们学校。 We welcome them to our school.
3　如果＋某人＋动词，…… 如果 + sb. + verb, ….	如果你有问题，你跟我联系。 If you have any question, you can contact me. 如果他有兴趣，可以看看我们的网页。 If he is interested, he can check out our web page.
4　除了……以外，还…… Besides … also ….	姐姐除了英语以外，还会法语。 Besides English, my sister can also speak French. 除了学习以外，他还在公司兼职。 Besides being a student, he also works part-time in a company.
5　虽然……，但是…… Although… (but) ….	课虽然很难，但是很有意思。 Although the class is difficult, it is still very interesting. 他虽然没做过导游，但是他有别的工作经验。 Although he has never been a tour guide before, he has other working experience.
6　某人＋来／去＋动词重叠。 Sb. + 来 / 去 + reduplicated verb.	你们来试试吧。 You should have a try. 我去准备准备。 I will go and prepare.

第一单元小结 Unit One Summary

7	时间词＋以前／以后，某人＋动词＋地方。 Time noun + 以前／以后, sb. + verb + somewhere.	一个月以前，他去上海了。 One month ago, he went to Shanghai. 半年以后，他就进了工厂。 After half a year, he went to the factory.
8	动词＋（名词）＋以后，某人＋动词。 Verb + (noun) + 以后, sb. + verb.	毕业以后，我想去旅行。 After graduation, I want to travel. 看了介绍以后，他申请了这个兼职工作。 After reading the introduction, he applied for the part-time job.
9	某人₁＋一……，某人₂＋就＋…… Sb.₁ + 一 ..., sb.₂ + 就 + ...	他一回来，我们就去看他。 When he comes back, we will go and see him. 老师一说考试，我们就紧张。 Every time the teacher mentions exams, we are very nervous.

第四课 Lesson

4

You Are Welcome to Our Community
欢迎你到我们社区来

Learning Objectives

交际话题 Topic of conversation:

社区环境 Environment in the
Shèqū huánjìng Community

基本句型 Sentence patterns:

住在这里的人多吗?

我出生的城市没有北京那么大。

我们社区有一个很大的广场。

New Words

1. 社区 shèqū n. community
2. 停 tíng v. to stop; to stop over
3. 一直 yìzhí adv. straight forward; all through
4. 住 zhù v. to live, to stay
5. 那么 nàme pron. like that; in that way; then
6. 房子 fángzi n. house, building
7. 博物馆 bówùguǎn n. museum
8. 天安门广场 Tiān'ānmén Guǎngchǎng n. Tian'anmen Square
9. 世界 shìjiè n. world, universe
10. 公园 gōngyuán n. park
11. 许多 xǔduō adj. many; a lot of

Text

Part I

大卫：老师，欢迎你来我们社区。
　　　　　　　　　　　　shèqū

老师：你们社区真大。我可以在这

　　　里停车吗？
　　　　tíng

大卫：不可以，一直走到前面就可
　　　　　　　yìzhí

　　　以停车了。

老师：这里的树真多，还有花园，

　　　真漂亮。

大卫：它是我们社区最大的花园。

老师：这个花园真大，有我们学

　　　校的花园大吗？

大卫：它没有学校的花园大，可是

　　　跟学校的花园一样漂亮。

老师：是，非常漂亮。住在这里的
　　　　　　　　　　　　zhù

　　　人多吗？

大卫：一到周末，这里的人就很多。

　　　别的时候，人没有那么多。
　　　　　　　　　　　nàme

老师：那个房子是图书馆吗？
　　　　　fángzi

大卫：不是，它是一个博物馆。我
　　　　　　　　　　bówùguǎn

　　　们社区有两个博物馆。这个

　　　是明信片博物馆，那边还有

　　　一个报纸博物馆。

老师：明信片博物馆？一定很有

　　　意思，我们可以去看看吗？

大卫：当然可以。里边有很多以前

　　　的明信片，很有趣。

老师：如果喜欢，可以买吗？

大卫：有的可以买。

我们社区有一个很大的广场

去年我第一次去了北京，我觉得北京太大了。我去了故宫、长城，还去了天安门广场 (Tiān'ānmén Guǎngchǎng)，它是世界 (shìjiè) 上最大的广场。我住在一个叫"花园"的社区里。它在北京的东边，旁边有一个非常大的城市公园 (gōngyuán)。社区里的房子都很漂亮，每个房子前边有一个小花园。社区里有一个图书馆，它不大。因为有许多 (xǔduō) 书可以看，所以这里是人们最喜欢去的地方。

我出生在中国南方 (nánfāng) 的一个小城市，虽然它没有北京大，可是很漂亮。那里有很多树，都很高很大，还有一些漂亮的公园。我住的社区就在城市的中心，它有一个好听的名字，叫"春风"社区。社区里有一个很大的广场，我常常在广场上玩儿。

北京的社区跟我们的社区不一样，我喜欢我们的社区，也喜欢北京的社区；我喜欢我出生的城市，也喜欢北京。

Exercises

 Read 1 Put a cross in the correct box according to Part I of the Text.

1) Where is David visiting?

A	B	C
A community	A garden	A school

2) What does David see a lot there?

A	B	C
Cars	Flowers	Trees

3) What is David talking about?

A	B	C
A library	A museum	A parking lot

Listen 2 Martin is talking about his sister's painting. Answer the following questions in English.

1) What is this painting about?

....

2) Are there many houses in her painting?

....

3) What is there around her house?

....

4) What is there in the square?

....

5) What is next to my home?

....

Read
3

Put a cross to the five correct answers according to Part II of the text.

A I have been to Beijing before.

B I visited the biggest square in the world.

C I stayed in a community which was in the east part of Beijing.

D There are many big museums in that community.

E I've seen many interesting things in those museums.

F The city I was born is not as big as Beijing.

G There are many big trees in my city.

H We often play in the square in the city centre.

Talk
4

Read the following paragraph and answer the questions below in Chinese.

　　我住在这个城市的西边，从市中心到我家不太远。虽然我住的社区不大，但是很漂亮。社区里有一条小河，河的两边都是树和花。夏天的时候，我们最喜欢在河边玩儿。社区里还有一个很大的广场，我们有的时候在广场上看电影。广场旁边有一个很小的房子，那是一个社区电影票博物馆，我觉得这大概（dàgài, probably）是世界上最小的博物馆。那里有许多电影票，除了中国的以外，还有外国的。我们的房子也都很漂亮。欢迎你到我们社区来，你一定会喜欢这里。

1) Where is this community?

....

2) Is it a very big community?

....

3) Where do 'we' usually play in summer?

....

4) Where do 'we' watch films?

....

5) What kind of museum do 'we' have?

....

Talk 5 You are going to talk about your community. You will talk about:

1) Where it is.   2) The environment.

3) The buildings.   4) Basic facilities.

5) What you think about it.

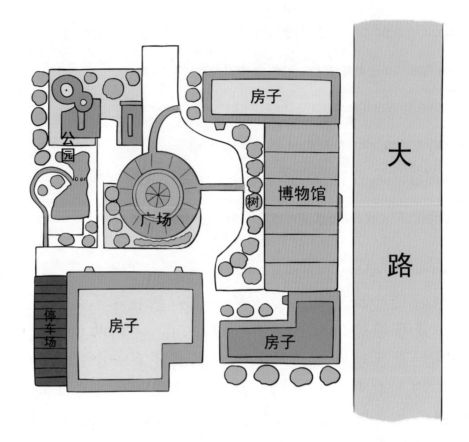

Write 6

Essay Plan Form

Essay title:

You want to help your parents to decide which community you're going to move to.

1) Compare the location

2) Compare the environment

3) Compare the houses

4) Which one you prefer

5) Special advantages of the one you prefer

Your conclusion

Read 7 Reorganize the following sentences and create a short paragraph.

1）我去了故宫、长城，还去了天安门广场，它是世界上最大的广场。

2）社区里的房子都很漂亮，每个房子前边有一个花园。

3）去年我第一次去了北京，我觉得北京太大了。

4）社区里有一个图书馆，它不大，但是它是人们最喜欢去的地方。

5）我住在一个叫"花园"的社区里，它在北京的东边。

6）"花园"社区的旁边有一个非常大的城市公园。

第五课 Lesson

5

I Live in This Neighbourhood As Well
我也住在这个社区

Learning Objectives

交际话题 Topic of conversation:

社区设施 Facilities in the
Shèqū shèshī Community

基本句型 Sentence patterns:

我也住在这个社区。
学校离我家很近。
我和你先去买邮票，再
一起去图书馆。

New Words

1 免费 miǎnfèi v. to be free

2 游泳池 yóuyǒngchí n. swimming pool

3 邮局 yóujú n. post office

4 邮票 yóupiào n. postage stamp

5 寄 jì v. to send, to post

6 收到 shōudào v. to receive, to accept

7 湖 hú n. lake

8 座 zuò m.w. (a measure word used mostly for large or fixed objects, e.g. mountains, bridges)

9 桥 qiáo n. bridge

10 散步 sànbù v. to go for a walk or stroll

11 离 lí v. to be away from; to leave; to part from

12 教堂 jiàotáng n. church, temple, cathedral

Text

Part I

本： 玛丽，这是你拍的照片吗？

玛丽：不是，这是我买的明信片。因为这张明信片上有我家的房子。

本： 是吗？在哪里？

玛丽：你看，这个房子就是我家。我是在社区博物馆买的这张明信片。

本： 是"东华"社区吧？我也住
Dōnghuá
在这个社区。

玛丽：对，就是"东华"社区。我

不知道你也住在这里。我觉得这个社区很漂亮。

本： 我也很喜欢这里，花园特别美，还有一个免费的游泳池。你
miǎnfèi　　yóuyǒngchí
常常去吗？

玛丽：我不会游泳。我常常去社区博物馆。

本： 我们的图书馆也很好，有很多书，还有电脑。我常常去那里看书、上网。

玛丽：你什么时候去图书馆？我和你一起去，好吗？

本： 我正打算现在就去。

玛丽：可是我现在要去邮局买邮票。
yóujú　　yóupiào

本： 没关系。我和你先去买邮票，再一起去图书馆，怎么样？

玛丽：好极了，走吧！

市中心有邮局、图书馆和超市

大海：

你好！

你寄（jì）来的照片我收到（shōudào）了，谢谢！你们家真漂亮，你们的社区也很漂亮。你什么时候来英国？欢迎你来我家。

我住在一个小城市，我家离（lí）市中心不太远。那里有邮局、图书馆和超市，还有博物馆和银行。周末的时候市中心很热闹。我最喜欢那里的小湖（hú），湖上有一座桥（zuò qiáo）。我们常常在桥上玩儿，还在桥上看湖里的鱼。湖边有一个大花园，常常有人在那里散步（sànbù）、休息。

我家附近有教堂（jiàotáng）、超市、图书馆和一个学校。我和妹妹都在这个学校上学。因为这里没有太多学生，中学毕业以后，我们就要去市中心的大学学习，也有的学生去别的城市上大学。社区里还有一个免费的游泳池，我常常去那儿游泳。我知道你很喜欢游泳，你来我家的时候，我们一起去吧。

你的朋友：Sam

2014年5月6日

Exercises

Read 1 Put a cross in the correct box according to Part I of the Text.

1) What are they talking about?

A	B	C
A picture	A painting	A postcard

2) Which of the following is for free?

A	B	C
Swimming pool	Postcard	Stamp

3) Where are they going first?

A	B	C
Museum	Post office	Library

Listen 2 A woman is showing us a map of a housing estate. Answer the following questions in English.

1) How many gates are there?

....

2) Where is the garden?

....

3) What do they have around the square?

....

4) What other facilities are available?

....

5) What is her comment on the housing estate?

....

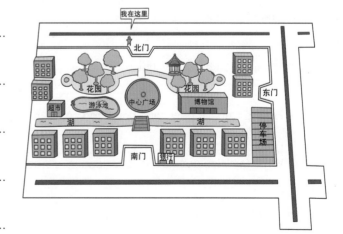

Read 3 Put a cross to the five correct answers according to Part II of the Text.

A Sam has received the pictures Dahai sent him.

B Sam's city is not as big as Dahai's.

C There is a bridge across the lake in the centre of the city.

D There is a big garden next to the river.

E Sam's house is far from the centre of the city.

F There is a church in Sam's community.

G The school is close to Sam's house.

H There is a free swimming pool in the centre of the city.

Talk 4 Read the following paragraph and answer the questions below in Chinese.

Sam,

我寄给你的照片收到了吗？那些是我新家的照片。我的新家离市中心很远，在一个新的社区里。这个社区虽然没有我以前的社区那么大，但是比以前的社区漂亮。社区里有超市，还有邮局、图书馆和游泳池。游泳池是免费的，我常常去。我最喜欢社区里的湖，湖里有很多鱼，湖上还有一座桥，很多人在桥上散步、玩儿，这里是我认识新朋友的好地方。

大海

1) What has Dahai sent to Sam?

....

2) Where is Dahai's new house?

....

3) How is Dahai's new neighbourhood compared to the previous one?

....

4) What facilities does Dahai's residential district have there?

....

5) Why does Dahai like the lake?

....

Talk
5

You are going to talk about your favourite part of the neighbourhood. You will talk about:

1) Where you live.

2) Available facilities.

3) Your favourite facility.

4) Your reason.

5) What you usually do with it.

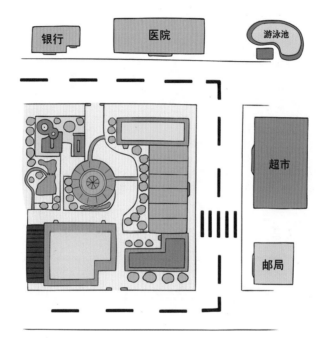

Write
6

Essay Plan Form

Essay title:

A letter to your Chinese friend telling him/her about your neighbourhood.

1) Your city and your country

2) Location of your house

3) Environment of your neighbourhood

4) Available facilities

5) What you usually do in your neighbourhood

6) How you like it

7) Asking about his/her neighbourhood

Your conclusion

Read 7 Reorganize the following sentences and create a short paragraph.

1）市中心有邮局、图书馆和超市，还有博物馆和银行。

2）我家附近有教堂、超市、图书馆和一个学校。我和妹妹都在这个学校上学。

3）我住在一个小城市的北边，离市中心不太远。

4）我最喜欢市中心的小湖，湖上有一座桥。我们常常在桥上玩儿。

5）社区里还有一个免费的游泳池，你来我家的时候，我们一起去吧。

6）周末的时候，市中心很热闹。

7）湖边有一个大花园，常常有人在那里散步、休息。

第六课 Lesson **6**

I Am Very Fond of This Community
我很喜欢这个社区

Learning Objectives

交际话题 Topic of conversation:

社区设施 Facilities in the
Shèqū shèshī Community

基本句型 Sentence patterns:

这个社区虽然不大，但是
我住得很舒服。
社区里空气新鲜，交通
和购物都很方便。
博物馆里面有许多古代
的东西。

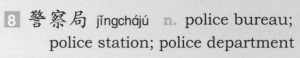

New Words

1 舒服 shūfu **adj.** comfortable
2 环境 huánjìng **n.** environment, circumstances
3 方便 fāngbiàn **adj.** convenient
4 空气 kōngqì **n.** air
5 交通 jiāotōng **n.** traffic, transportation
6 办公室 bàngōngshì **n.** office
7 百货公司 bǎihuò gōngsī **n.** department store

8 警察局 jǐngchájú **n.** police bureau; police station; police department
9 古代 gǔdài **n.** ancient times
10 地铁 dìtiě **n.** subway, underground, tube
11 十分 shífēn **adv.** very, fully
12 或者 huòzhě **conj.** or

Text

Part I

大明：大卫，你到北京以后住在哪儿？

大卫：我住在"湖边"社区。

大明："湖边"社区？离市中心远吗？

大卫：很远。

大明：为什么住在那么远的地方？

大卫：因为我在这个社区教英语，所以就住在这里了。

大明：那个社区怎么样？

大卫：非常好。这个社区虽然不大，但是我住得很舒服。
shūfu

大明：环境怎么样？方便吗？
huánjìng　　　fāngbiàn

大卫：社区里空气新鲜，交通和
kōngqì　　　jiāotōng
购物都很方便。
fāngbiàn

大明：有游泳的地方吗？

大卫：有，游泳池还是免费的，我常常去。

大明：那真好。你什么时候来市中心？欢迎你到我的办公室
bàngōngshì
来看看。

大卫：你的办公室还在花园路59号吗？

大明：还在那儿，在市中心电影院旁边。

大卫：好的，我一定去。

我很喜欢这个社区

周老师：

您好！

我来北京已经两个月了，我很喜欢这里。我认识了很多新朋友，也去了很多新地方。

现在我住在朋友家里，他家在北京西边的一个很漂亮的社区里。这里环境非常好，有很多树和花。人们都说，这里是北京空气最新鲜的地方。这个社区虽然不大，但是大家住得很舒服。社区里除了超市、银行，还有百货公司、图书馆和公园，离警察局和邮局都不很远。社区上网也十分方
bǎihuò gōngsī   jǐngchájú   shífēn
便，我常常在网上跟爸爸妈妈聊天儿。

这里的人没有市中心那么多，所以不太热闹。有的时候我们去市中心电影院看电影，还去书店买书。市中心有一个很大的博物馆，叫中国国家博物馆，里面有很多古代的东西，我很感兴趣。从朋友家到市中心的交通
                              gǔdài
也非常方便，坐公共汽车或者地铁都可以到。周老师，您什么时候来北
                    huòzhě dìtiě
京？一定来这里看看。

您的学生：大卫

Exercises

Read 1 Put a cross in the correct box according to Part 1 of the text.

1) Where does David live now?

A	B	C
Lakeside Residential District	City centre	Centre Road

2) What does David think about that place?

A	B	C
Very big	Very comfortable	Not that convenient

3) What is it at No.59 Garden Road?

A	B	C
A cinema	A swimming pool	Daming's office

Listen 2 Sam is talking about his new idea. Answer the following questions in English.

1) What does he think about the city centre?

....

2) Why does he want to find a house in the north part of the city?

....

3) What is there in the north part of the city?

....

4) What is he going to do?

....

5) What is he looking forward to?

....

Read
3

Put a cross to the five correct answers according to Part II of the Text.

A David has been in Beijing for two weeks.

B David is staying in a friend's place in the west part of Beijing.

C This neighbourhood is not big but it's very comfortable and convenient.

D There are banks and department stores but there is no police station in this compound.

E The Internet service is very convenient.

F It's not as busy as it is in the city centre.

G National Museum of China is located in the city centre.

H The transportation is not that convenient from this neighbourhood to the city.

Talk
4

Read the following paragraph and answer the questions below in Chinese.

　　因为爸爸要到别的城市工作，所以我们打算搬家（bānjiā，to move）。我们在网上看了许多小区的介绍。爸爸希望找一个空气新鲜、环境好的；妈妈希望找一个干净、舒服、购物方便的；我和妹妹觉得交通方便最重要，离市中心不要太远。今天妹妹在网上看到一个小区的照片，这个小区叫西山（Xīshān，Western Hills）小区，在城市的西边。它离市中心不远，房子很大，小区里有很多树和花，除了有超市、银行、图书馆、停车场以外，还有免费的博物馆和游泳池。学校、警察局和百货公司都不很远。我们每个人都很满意。

1) Why do 'we' want to move?

....

2) What requirements do the parents have?

....

3) What are the children's requirements?

....

4) Which is the one 'we' all like?

....

5) What facilities do 'we' have in this neighbourhood?

....

Talk 5 You are discussing with your parents about moving to a new community. Tell them about your concern. You will talk about:

1) Your comments on your present house.

2) The reason your want to move.

3) The most important aspect.

4) The second most important aspect.

5) What you don't care too much about.

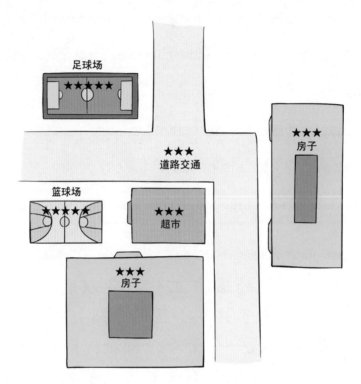

Write 6

Essay Plan Form

Essay title:

A letter to the estate manager asking about the neighbourhood.

1) You're interested in this neighbourhood.

2) Ask about the environment

3) Ask about the facilities

4) One special aspect you are concerned about

5) Ask about other residents' comments

6) You wish to receive his/her reply

Your conclusion

Read 7 Reorganize the following sentences and create a short paragraph.

1）这里环境非常好，有许多树和花。

2）现在我住在一个朋友家里，他家在北京西边一个很漂亮的社区里。

3）从社区到市中心的交通非常方便，坐公共汽车或地铁都可以到。我很喜欢这个社区。

4）我来北京已经两个月了，我很喜欢这里，还认识了很多新朋友。

5）在社区上网也十分方便，我常常在网上跟爸爸妈妈聊天儿。

6）社区里除了超市、银行，还有百货公司、图书馆和小公园，我家离警察局和邮局也不远。

苏州园林

　　苏州古典园林的历史很悠久，到16～18世纪是全盛时期，苏州至今保存尚好的古典园林有数十处，并因此使苏州享有"人间天堂"的美誉。苏州园林的特点与北京的皇家园林不同，作为苏州古典园林典型的拙政园、留园、网师园等，构筑精巧，亭台楼阁错落有致，体现出江南景色精致、秀美的特征。

Classical Gardens of Suzhou

The classical gardens of Suzhou are a group of gardens in Suzhou City, Jiangsu Province. Garden building in Suzhou reached its height during the 16th and 18th centuries. Dozens of gardens in and around Suzhou are still in good condition, giving the city a reputation of being "paradise on earth". Humble Administrator's Garden, Lingering Garden, and Master of the Nets Garden represent the art of Suzhou-style classical gardens. Different from the imperial gardens in Beijing, Suzhou gardens are noted for their exquisite design and layout, presenting an image of delicate and multifarious buildings of old times in the southern region of the lower Yangtze River.

第二单元小结   Unit Two Summary

1	A＋ 没有 ＋ B（＋ 那么）＋ 形容词。 A ＋ 没有 ＋B（＋ 那么）＋ adjective.	我没有哥哥高。 I am not as tall as my brother. 这个城市没有北京那么大。 This city is not as big as Beijing.
2	某人＋住＋在＋某处。 Sb. ＋ 住 ＋ 在 ＋ somewhere.	她住在妈妈家。 She lives with her mother. 我们住在这个社区。 We live in this neighbourhood.
3	某人＋什么时候＋动词词组? Sb. ＋ 什么时候 ＋ verb phrase?	他们什么时候去旅行? When will they travel? 你什么时候去买邮票? When will you go buy stamps?
4	名词₁＋离＋名词₂＋ 形容词。 Noun₁ ＋ 离 ＋ noun₂ ＋ adjective.	大学离我家很近。 My college is very close to my home. 邮局离超市不太远。 The post office is not very far away from the supermarket.
5	某处＋有＋名词₁、名词₂＋和＋名词₃。 Somewhere ＋ 有 ＋ noun₁, noun₂ ＋ and ＋ noun₃.	市中心有教堂、广场和博物馆。 There is a church, a public square and a museum in the city centre. 房子前边有树、花和草。 There are trees, flowers and grass in front of the house.
6	某人＋来／去＋动词词组。 Sb. ＋ 来／去 ＋ verb phrases.	我去邮局买邮票。 I went to the post office to buy stamps. 你来我家听音乐。 You can come to my house to listen to music.

第二单元小结　Unit Two　Summary

7	名词（某处）＋不＋很＋形容词。 Somewhere ＋ 不 ＋ 很 ＋ adjective.	他说得不很清楚。 What he said is not very clear. 警察局离这儿不很远。 The police station is not far away from here.
8	一直＋动词（词组）。 Keep ＋ verb (phrase).	一直走。 Keep walking. 一直往前开。 Keep driving.

第七课 Lesson **7**

It's Good for Your Health to Eat More Vegetables and Fruits
多吃蔬菜、水果对身体好

Learning Objectives

交际话题 Topic of conversation:

健康的饮食 Healthy Food
Jiànkāng de yǐnshí

基本句型 Sentence patterns:

多吃蔬菜、水果对身体好。

他的身体还是那么好。

他很少吃肉、喝酒。

他喜欢和别的老人一起聊新闻。

我们都爱吃她做的点心。

New Words

1 肉 ròu **n.** meat
2 身体 shēntǐ **n.** body
3 筷子 kuàizi **n.** chopstick
4 餐厅 cāntīng **n.** restaurant
5 饿 è **adj.** hungry
6 瘦 shòu **adj.** thin, slim
7 太太 tàitai **n.** wife
8 睡觉 shuìjiào **v.** to have a sleep

9 酒 jiǔ **n.** wine, alcohol
10 渴 kě **adj.** thirsty
11 老人 lǎorén **n.** senior
12 汤 tāng **n.** soup
13 爱 ài **v.** to like, to love
14 端午节 Duānwǔ Jié **n.** Dragon Boat Festival
15 粽子 zòngzi **n.** Zongzi (a traditional food eaten in Dragon Boat Festival)

Text

Part I

本： 你们看，今天的天气多好！

小雨： 是啊，今天我们来公园太合适了。看我准备的这些好吃的东西。

本： 没有肉啊！你不喜欢吃
ròu
肉吗？

小雨： 喜欢，可是今天我不想吃。你准备了什么？

本： 我准备了鸡肉，也有一些蔬菜、水果。多吃蔬菜、水果对身体好。
shēntǐ

丽丽： 我这里有海鲜，你看，这是鱼。你们喜不喜欢吃鱼？

本： 当然喜欢。我妈妈常常做鱼给我们吃。

小雨： 电影院的附近有一个餐厅，
cāntīng
那里的鱼好吃极了，我和爸

爸妈妈去过。

丽丽： 是吗？我也想去。

小雨： 那是一个中国餐厅。你会用
筷子了吗？
kuàizi

丽丽： 会，我现在用筷子用得很好。

小雨： 那好。那个餐厅里有很多蔬菜，还有鸡肉、鸭肉、牛肉和猪肉，我都觉得很好吃。那里的汤也很好喝。
tāng

本： 不要说了，我们现在开始吃吧，我已经很饿了。
è

祝王先生和王太太的身体健康

王先生今年虽然75岁了，但是他的身体还是那么好，不胖也不

瘦。他每天早上6点就起来跑步，上午还去公园散步，晚上差不多
shòu

10点睡觉。他很少吃肉、喝酒，喜欢吃蔬菜和水果，渴了就喝水和
    shuìjiào   jiǔ   kě

茶。

王先生虽然是一个老人，可是他对许多事情都感兴趣。他常常
            lǎorén

看报纸，喜欢和别的老人一起聊新闻。他还喜欢旅行，喜欢认识新

朋友。

王太太人也很好，她常常请朋友去她家里。她做的点心特别好
    tàitài

吃，我们都爱吃她做的点心。端午节要到了，她说这个周末给我们
        ài   Duānwǔ Jié

包粽子吃。我们准备一起庆祝，也祝王先生和王太太的身体健康。
    zòngzi

Exercises

Read 1 Put a cross in the correct box according to Part I of the text.

1) What does Ben bring today?

A	B	C
Pork	Fish	Chicken

2) Where is the Chinese restaurant?

A	B	C
Near a cinema	Near the railway station	In a cinema

3) What is the dish that Xiaoyu didn't mention?

A	B	C
Beef	Lamb	Duck

Listen 2 You are listening to an introduction of a restaurant. Answer the following questions in English.

1) How do they know about the restaurant?

....

2) Why does the father like to go to this restaurant?

....

3) What dishes are there in this restaurant?

....

4) What are the dishes made of?

....

5) What do they think about the prices?

....

Read
3

Put a cross to the five correct answers according to Part Ⅱ of the text.

A Mr. Wang likes to have a run or walk every morning.

B Mr. Wang watches TV news until 10 o'clock in the evening.

C Mr. Wang seldom drinks alcohol.

D Mr. Wang likes to learn new things very much.

E Mr. Wang cannot travel because he is very old.

F Mrs. Wang often cooks meat for Mr. Wang because he likes it.

G We all like the desserts that Mrs. Wang made.

H We wish Mr. and Mrs. Wang a very healthy life.

Talk
4

Read the following paragraph and answer the questions below in Chinese.

　　我的家人常常喝茶。我在很小的时候就看爸爸妈妈喝茶：春天喝茉莉花茶(mòlìhuāchá，jasmine tea)；夏天很热，喝绿茶；秋天喝乌龙茶(wūlóngchá，oolong tea)；冬天喝红茶。开始的时候我觉得茶不好喝，我更喜欢喝果汁和汽水。可是我大了以后，看了很多新闻，也和一些朋友聊天儿，知道茶是很好的饮料，对人的身体很好。我们去中国旅行的时候，很多地方都有很特别的茶。我们买了一些试试，好喝极了。我最喜欢喝花茶，喝茶用的茶杯(chábēi，tea cup)也很漂亮，让我觉得很有中国的特色(tèsè，character)。

1) What do 'we' usually drink?

....

2) Can you try to give the names of the different types of tea?

....

3) Why did 'I' start to like tea?

....

4) What did 'we' do when 'we' travelled in China?

....

5) What do 'I' think about drinking tea?

....

Talk 5 You are going to talk about your daily life with a friend. You will talk about:

1) The time to get up and go to bed, and why.
2) Favourite sport or activity.
3) Good places to do physical exercise.
4) Favourite food.
5) Food or drink that you don't like and why.
6) Favourite courses.

Write 6

Essay Plan Form

Essay title:

You ask your friend to take care of your pet, such as a dog, a cat or etc. during your 2 week's travel. Write him/her a note to tell him/her what to do.

1) Your pet's name

2) Your pet's favourite food

3) Time and amount of feeding

4) Your pet's favourite activities

5) Place or time of sleeping

6) What to do if your pet is sick

Your conclusion

Read
7

Reorganize the following sentences and create a short paragraph.

1）他每天早上6点就起来跑步，上午还去公园散步。

2）王先生虽然是一个老人，可是他对许多事情都感兴趣。

3）王太太做的点心特别好吃，我们都爱吃她做的点心。

4）他晚上差不多10点睡觉。

5）她说这个周末给我们包粽子吃。

6）王先生今年虽然75岁了，但是他的身体还是那么好，不胖也不瘦。

第八课　Lesson **8**

I Want to Take Some Pictures of a Panda
我要拍一些熊猫的照片

Learning Objectives

交际话题 Topic of conversation:

休闲活动 Leisure Activities
Xiūxián huódòng

基本句型 Sentence patterns:
从伦敦到北京坐飞机去要几个小时？
大约要十个小时。
有时候我们从早上一直玩到晚上。

New Words

1 暑假 shǔjià **n.** summer holiday
2 大约 dàyuē **adv.** about, approximately
3 参观 cānguān **v.** to visit
4 动物园 dòngwùyuán **n.** zoo
5 熊猫 xióngmāo **n.** panda
6 西山 Xīshān **n.** Western Hills

7 海 hǎi **n.** sea
8 休闲 xiūxián **adj.** leisure
9 船 chuán **n.** boat, ship
10 滑冰 huá bīng **n./v.** skating; to skate
11 等等 děngděng **part.** etc.; and so on
12 快乐 kuàilè **adj.** happy

Text

Part I

（本和玛丽在网上聊天儿。）

本：　　真高兴，快放暑假了。
　　　　　　　　　　shǔjià

玛丽：我跟你一样，也特别高兴。

　　　　你放暑假后有什么计划?

本：　　我想到中国去旅行。

玛丽：是吗? 你要从英国到中国去

　　　　旅行?

本：　　是的，我要和爸爸妈妈一起

　　　　去北京看长城。

玛丽：从伦敦到北京坐飞机去要几

　　　　个小时?

本：　　大约要十个小时。
　　　　dàyuē

玛丽：除了长城以外，你们还想去

　　　　哪儿?

本：　　北京有许多博物馆，我们

　　　　准备去参观故宫。北京也
　　　　　　　cānguān

　　　　有很多公园和购物中心，

　　　　我们都想去看看。

玛丽：你去动物园吗?
　　　　　　dòngwùyuán

本：　　当然! 我还要拍一些熊 猫
　　　　　　　　　　　　　　　xióngmāo

　　　　的照片。

玛丽：太好了，一定要给我们看看。

本：　　我可以发给你看。

玛丽：到了北京以后，你要和我

　　　　联系。

本：　　会的。我会给你打电话，

　　　　或者写电子邮件。

我有很多休闲活动
xiūxián

　　我家住在北京的西山附近，那里的空气非常好，有许多树和草，
Xīshān

山下还有公园。那里没有海，只有一条河。
hǎi

　　我上中学的时候有很多休闲活动。春天来了，草绿了，花红了，

我和同学去山上或者河边玩，有时候我们从早上一直玩到晚上。夏天
huòzhě

天气很热，公园里有船，我们就在船上一边聊天儿一边唱歌。秋天天
chuán

气最好，我们从山上能看得很远，风景非常漂亮。到了冬天，我们就

去滑冰。下雪的时候，我们会去长城拍照片。
huá bīng

　　我的休闲活动还有很多。有时候我们去动物园。我最喜欢看熊

猫，它们都可爱极了。我们也听音乐、看电影、做运动等等。我对流
děngděng

行音乐很感兴趣，常买一些音乐CD听。有时候我和同学上网订流行音

乐会的票。我的中学生活非常快乐。
kuàilè

Exercises

Read 1 Put a cross in the correct box according to Part I of the text.

1) What is the reason that Ben is so happy?

A	B	C
Weekend	Vacation	Party

2) Where is Ben going to see the Great Wall?

A	B	C
On the Internet	In a picture	In Beijing

3) What is the place that Ben didn't mention?

A	B	C
Museum	Zoo	City centre

Listen 2 You are listening to a girl telling a story about her mother. Answer the following questions in English.

1) What does her mother do in school?

....

2) What does her mother do at home?

....

3) Can you list four to five hobbies of her mother's?

....

4) Does her mother have more time than others? What does she look like?

....

5) What does the girl think about her mother?

....

Read 3 Put a cross to the five correct answers according to Part Ⅱ of the text.

A He lives near the Western Hills.

B The view is beautiful there.

C He likes to row boats with classmates in summer.

D The winter is so cold there that he can find nothing fun to do.

E He likes snow.

F He is interested in popular music.

G He books tickets for concerts on the Internet sometimes.

H His life in middle school is too busy for him to have free time.

Talk 4 Read the following paragraph and answer the questions below in Chinese.

　　山山的爸爸是一名医生，每天工作十多个小时，常常工作到很晚，有时候周末也没有空儿休息。爸爸说他很想运动，可是因为太累了，所以总是想睡觉。他看电视的时候，也想睡觉。山山不知道有什么好办法可以帮助他。爸爸也常常上网，那也是因为工作。山山说，他常看见爸爸在电脑前边坐四五个小时，他觉得这对爸爸的身体不好。周末妈妈买了一个跑步机，他们希望爸爸可以多运动。

1) What is the job of Shanshan's father?

2) Does his father want to exercise?

3) What does his father use the Internet for?

4) How would you describe his father's health?

5) What did they buy for his father and why?

Talk 5

You are going to talk about leisure activities with a friend. You will talk about:

1) Facilities near your home such as a swimming pool, football field or basketball court, park, cinema, etc.

2) Any club you are in.

3) The time when you participate in the activities.

4) Your opinions about health, happiness, friendship and so on.

5) Suggestions to your friend.

Write 6

Essay Plan Form

Essay title:

Write a note to a research group which is conducting a survey about secondary school student's summer holiday.

1) Places you visited

2) Movie or show you watched

3) New skill you learned

4) New things you tried

5) Your feeling about the above activities

6) Your plan for next holiday

Your conclusion

Reorganize the following sentences and create a short paragraph.

Read 7

1）夏天天气很热，公园里有船，我们在船上一边聊天儿，一边唱歌。

2）我的休闲活动还有听音乐、看电影等等。

3）秋天天气最好，我们去山上玩。

4）我家住在北京的西山附近，那里的空气非常好。

5）春天的时候，草绿了，花红了。

6）到了冬天，我们就去滑冰。下雪的时候我们会去长城拍照片。

第九课 **Lesson** **9**

I'm Not Feeling Well
我病了

Learning Objectives

交际话题 Topic of conversation:

看医生 Seeing a Doctor
Kàn yīshēng

基本句型 Sentence patterns:

我给你做个检查吧。

你生病了，就应该在家休息。

吃药以后，感冒就会很快好吗？

New Words

1 眼睛 yǎnjing **n.** eye

2 片 piàn **m.w.** (a measure word used for pills)

3 量 liáng **v.** to check

4 一下 yíxià one time

5 检查 jiǎnchá **n./v.** check; to check

6 体温 tǐwēn **n.** temperature

7 应该 yīnggāi **v.** should; ought to

8 药 yào **n.** medicine

9 穿 chuān **v.** to wear

10 衣服 yīfu **n.** clothes

11 年轻人 niánqīngrén **n.** young people

12 带 dài **v.** to bring, to take

13 宠物 chǒngwù **n.** pet

14 小朋友 xiǎopéngyou **n.** child

Text

Part I

大海：医生，我病了。

医生：你怎么了？

大海：我头疼、咳嗽，眼睛也不
　　　yǎnjing
　　　舒服。

医生：什么时候开始的？

大海：昨天晚上，差不多一天了。

医生：我给你做个检查吧，先量
　　　　　　　　jiǎnchá　　　liáng
　　　一下你的体温，看看体温
　　　yíxià　　　tǐwēn
　　　高不高。（量体温后）体温
　　　不太高，应该是感冒。

大海：明天我能不能去上课？

医生：你生病了，就应该在家
　　　　　　　　　　yīnggāi
　　　休息。

大海：可是明天我们有考试，我
　　　想我应该去学校。

医生：我给你一些药吧。
　　　　　　　　yào

大海：吃药以后，感冒就会很快

好吗？

医生：应该会好一些。除了吃药，
　　　你还要多喝水，多休息。

大海：谢谢医生。明天的考试很
　　　重要，我准备了很久。

医生：所以你一定要去学校，是吧？
　　　明天天气不好，你多穿一些
　　　　　　　　　　　　chuān
　　　衣服吧。
　　　yīfu

大海：好的，谢谢。

他们天天都去广场做运动

　　我们社区有一个很大的广场。广场的北边是一片绿绿的草地，草
pian
地中心有一个小小的湖。这里的环境很漂亮，空气也非常好。每天早上

有许多老人来这里跑步、打羽毛球、唱歌、跳舞。虽然很多人七十多岁

了，有几个人已经九十岁了，可是他们天天都去广场做运动，身体特别

健康。有一些老人还带他们的宠物一起出来活动。除了运动，他们还
　　　　　　　　　dài　　　　chǒngwù

一起聊天儿，聊电视新闻和一些新鲜的事情。

　　有时候我和同学们也去那里运动，和他们一起打球，他们很欢迎我

们。有的老人比我打得还好。这些老年人都喜欢运动，也喜欢交流，他

们每天都很快乐。除了老人以外，也有一些工作的年轻人到广场散步、
　　　　　　　　　　　　　　　　　　　　　niánqīngrén
做休闲活动。许多小朋友也常常在广场上跑步和玩儿。社区广场是我们
　　　　　　xiǎopéngyǒu
都喜欢去的地方。

Exercises

Read 1 Put a cross in the correct box according to Part I of the text.

1) When did Dahai feel sick?

A	B	C
Yesterday morning	Yesterday evening	Today

2) Can Dahai go to school tomorrow?

A	B	C
Yes, there is no problem at all.	Yes, but he needs rest.	No, he needs a good rest.

3) Why does Dahai want to go to school?

A	B	C
An important sports match	An important test	An interesting class

Listen 2 You are listening to a boy talking about his feelings. Answer the following questions in English.

1) How does he feel? For how long?

....

2) Does he want to see the doctor? Why?

....

3) What do they want to do this week?

....

4) What does he want to have now? Why?

....

5) How does he feel during vacation?

....

Read 3 Put a cross to the five correct answers according to Part Ⅱ of the text.

A There is a lake near his house.

B There are many young people who play sports in the morning.

C The old people like to communicate with others.

D Sometimes young students play with the old people .

E The old people dislike playing with the young students.

F Some old people can play better than the young students.

G There are more old people in the morning and more children in the evening.

H Not all of the people there like the community square.

Talk 4 Read the following paragraph and answer the questions below in Chinese.

这个周末同学们要一起去附近的山上玩，我们已经准备了一个星期，要在那儿吃东西，做游戏，唱歌。可是从昨天晚上开始，我的身体有点儿不舒服，体温有点儿高，头有点儿疼，不想吃饭。今天下午一个同学打电话来问我去不去玩，我告诉他先看看明天怎么样，如果不好，我就去看医生。离周末还有两天，我希望我的身体快快好。

1) What do 'we' plan to do this weekend?

....

2) What's wrong with 'me'? For how long?

....

3) Why did 'my' classmate give 'me' a phone call?

....

4) What did 'I' tell the classmate?

....

5) What is 'my' wish now?

....

Talk 5

You and one of your classmates will partner up to play doctor and patient. He/She is a doctor now and you will be the patient. You will talk about:

1）When you start to feel bad.

2）Tell the doctor your symptoms.

3）He/She will give some advice and suggestions such as "have a rest, have more vegetables and fruits", etc.

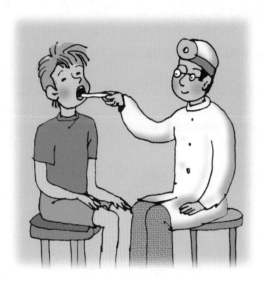

Essay Plan Form

Essay title:

A note to your Chinese teacher to ask for a day off.

1) You feel bad

2) When and what happened

3) Ask for a day off and tell him/her your plan

4) Ask if there is any homework

5) Ask what he/she will teach in Class in order to prepare if you feel good enough to return

Your conclusion

Read
7

Reorganize the following sentences and create a short paragraph.

1）除了运动，他们还一起聊天儿，聊电视新闻和一些新鲜的事情。

2）我们社区有一个很大的广场，每天早上有许多老年人在这里跑步、打羽毛球、唱歌、跳舞。

3）他们很欢迎我们。

4）虽然很多人七十多岁了，有几个人已经九十岁了，可是他们天天都到广场做运动，身体特别健康。

5）有时候我跟同学们也去那里运动，和他们一起打球。

6）除了老人以外，也有一些工作的年轻人晚上到广场散步、做休闲活动。

长江与黄河

　　长江是中国第一大河，发源于青藏高原，流经青海、四川、西藏、云南、湖北、湖南、江西等地，最后流入东海。长江全长6397千米，是世界第三长河。黄河全长约5464公里，流域面积约79.5万平方公里，是中国第二长河，世界第五大长河。在中国历史上，黄河流域给中华文明带来了巨大的影响，是中华民族最主要的发源地之一，被中国人称为"母亲河"。

Yangtze River and Yellow River

The Yangtze River, at 6,397 kilometres, is the longest river in China and the third-longest in the world. It flows from glaciers in the Qinghai-Tibet Plateau through Qinghai, Sichuan, Tibet, Yunnan, Hubei, Hunan, and Jiangxi, finally emptying into the East China Sea.

The Yellow River, at 5,464 kilometres, is the second-longest river in China and the fifth-longest in the world. Its total basin area is 795,000 square kilometres. The Yellow River is also called "the Mother River" as its basin was the birthplace of ancient Chinese civilisations and the most prosperous region throughout Chinese history.

第三单元小结　Unit Three Summary

1　多＋动词＋名词（＋补充词组）。 多 + verb + noun (+ complementary phrase).	多吃蔬菜。 Eat more vegetables. 多听音乐(对健康好)。 Listening to music is good for one's health.
2　名词(＋动宾词组)＋状态动词(这里用作副词)。 Noun (+ verb-object phrase) + stative verb (used as adverbs).	她做的点心也特别好吃。 She made very tasty dessert. 中文很难学。 Chinese is very difficult to learn.
3　从＋某处₁＋到＋某处₂＋要＋时间词。 从 + somewhere₁ + 到 + somewhere₂ + 要 + time noun.	从我家到学校要20分钟。 It took 20 minutes to get from my house to school. 从北京到伦敦要多长时间? How long does it take to get from Beijing to London?
4　动词＋一下（＋名词）。 Verb + 一下 (+ noun).	请看一下（这本书）。 Please read this book. 量一下体温吧。 Please take your temperature.
5　某人＋应该＋动词词组。 Sb. + 应该 + verb phrase.	你应该休息。 You should have a rest. 他们应该参加这个运动。 They should play this sport.
6　某人／物 ＋形容词＋了。 Sb./sth. + adjective + auxiliary word 了.	他胖了。 He has gained weight. 空气新鲜了。 The air is fresher.

第十课 Lesson **10**

My School
我的学校

New Words

1. 对 duì **adj.** right
2. 语言 yǔyán **n.** language
3. 懂 dǒng **v.** to know, to understand
4. 花 huā **v.** to spend
5. 记 jì **v.** to remember
6. 忘 wàng **v.** to forget
7. 越来越 yuèláiyuè more and more
8. 后来 hòulái **adv.** later
9. 要是 yàoshi **conj.** if
10. 错 cuò **adj.** wrong
11. 马上 mǎshàng **adv.** right away
12. 进步 jìnbù **n./v.** improvement; to improve
13. 参加 cānjiā **v.** to join
14. 练习 liànxí **n./v.** practice; to practise
15. 方法 fāngfǎ **n.** method, way

Text

Part I

（大卫去他的英国朋友Matthew家玩儿）

Matthew： 以前你来过这里吧？

大卫： 来过。我的一个中国同学住在这个社区，有时候我去他们家玩。

Matthew： 你和同学们说什么语言？
　　　　　　　　　　　yǔyán

大卫： 说汉语，也说英语。

Matthew： 我听过你说汉语，你的汉语说得比我好。你学习汉语多长时间了？

大卫： 我在英国的时候就学汉语。现在在中国，我天天说汉语。

Matthew： 你在学校都说汉语吗？

大卫： 不是。英国的同学跟我说汉语，中国的同学跟我说英语。

Matthew： 这很有意思。从你家到学校远吗？

大卫： 不远，骑自行车差不多要半个小时。

Matthew： 学校的课有趣吗？

大卫： 很有趣。我最喜欢中国地理课。我常常去地理课上学过的地方旅行。

Matthew： 旅行真是一个学习地理的好方法。
　　　　　　　　　　　　　　fāngfǎ

汉语不难学

今年春天我爸爸来到中国工作，所以我也开始在这里的学校学习。

学校里，除了我都是中国人。他们都说汉语，所以我也努力学习汉语。

开始的时候，我觉得汉语很难学，我听不懂老师和同学说什么。
dǒng

每天我花很多时间记汉字，写汉字，可是很快就忘了。后来天天听，
huā   jì   wàng   hòulái

天天说，我的汉语就越来越好了。现在我能和同学们说汉语了。要是我
yuèláiyuè   yàoshi

说错了，同学们马上就告诉我；要是我说对了，同学们都替我高兴。
cuò   mǎshàng   duì

现在我对汉语非常感兴趣，喜欢写汉字，也喜欢看中文电视节目，我的

汉语已经有了很大的进步。除了上课以外，我还常常参加学校的活动。
jìnbù   cānjiā

这个学期我们班要表演一个节目，同学们说要是我喜欢，就可以和他们

一起去练习。我当然很高兴参加了。
liànxí

Exercises

Read
1 Put a cross in the correct box according to Part I of the text.

1) In what language(s) do they speak when David talk with his Chinese classmate?

A	B	C
English	Chinese	Both English and Chinese

2) How long does it take to the school from David's home?

A	B	C
Half an hour	One hour	One and a half hour

3) What's David's favourite course in school?

A	B	C
History	Geography	Science

Listen
2 You are listening to a Chinese girl talking about her courses. Answer the following questions in English.

1) How does she feel today? Why?

....

2) Why does she like science?

....

3) Does she like P.E.? Why?

....

4) What's her problem with the course of English?

....

5) What will she do this weekend? Why?

....

Read 3

Put a cross to the five correct answers according to Part Ⅱ of the text.

A There are quite a lot of foreign students in this school.

B It's difficult for me to learn Chinese at the beginning.

C My Chinese characters are good because I spend a lot of time practising.

D I can speak Chinese very well now.

E I'm interested in Chinese and I'm making great progress.

F I cannot participate in activities because of my poor Chinese.

G I often participate in activities.

H My classmates asked me to join them to practise for the programme.

Talk 4

Read the following paragraph and answer the questions below in Chinese.

　　我家离学校很近，每天我走路去上课。我喜欢学校的课，也喜欢和同学们一起活动。我有三个好朋友，一个英语说得很好，一个数学学得最好，一个跑步跑得很快。我们下课常常在一起玩，回家以后还常常互相（hùxiāng，each other）打电话、问作业、聊天儿。我们的妈妈很高兴我们在一起，因为我们都很努力，进步也很大。马上要放假了，朋友们告诉我，他们要去学游泳和网球。我希望能和他们一起去。

1) How do 'I' get to school everyday?

....

2) What are 'my' best friends good at?

....

3) What do 'we' often do after going home?

....

4) Are 'our' mothers glad that 'we' are together? Why?

....

5) What are 'we' going to do during the vacation?

....

Talk 5

You are talking with a Chinese friend about your foreign language learning. You could mention:

1) When you started to learn.

2) The most difficult thing you encountered.

3) Your method that helps your learning.

4) Your level.

Write 6

Essay Plan Form

Essay title:
An email to describe your courses in school.

1) Names of the courses
2) Your favourite courses and why do you like it
3) Courses you dislike and the reason
4) The teachers
5) Homework and test

Your conclusion

Read 7 Reorganize the following sentences and create a short paragraph.

1) 现在我能和同学们说汉语了。

2) 学校里，除了我，都是中国人，他们都说汉语，所以我也努力学习汉语。

3) 我的汉语已经有了很大的进步。

4) 开始的时候，我觉得汉语很难学，我听不懂老师和同学说什么。

5) 现在我对汉语非常感兴趣，喜欢写汉字，也喜欢看中文电视节目。

6) 后来天天听，天天说，我的汉语就越来越好了。

11

Our Schools Are Sister Schools
我们两个学校是姐妹学校

Learning Objectives

交际话题 Topic of conversation:

学校之间的交流 Communication
Xuéxiào zhī jiān de jiāoliú Between Schools

基本句型 Sentence patterns:

我们两个学校是姐妹学校。
下个星期两个学校就有足球比赛。
比赛下午 4 点才开始。
网络上有许多免费的课程，让我
有机会学一些新东西。

New Words

1. 网友 wǎngyǒu **n.** net friend
2. 忙 máng **adj.** busy
3. 才 cái **adv.** then and only then
4. 再见 zàijiàn Goodbye.
5. 网络 wǎngluò **n.** the Internet
6. 有用 yǒuyòng **adj.** useful
7. 会 huì **v.** can; to be able to
8. 查看 chákàn **v.** to check; to look up
9. 无聊 wúliáo **adj.** boring
10. 让 ràng **v.** to let
11. 机会 jīhuì **n.** chance, opportunity
12. 生活 shēnghuó **n.** life

Text

Part I

（大海和小雨在网上用QQ聊天儿）

小雨：大海，你在网上吗？

大海：在。我正在和一个网友
　　　wǎngyǒu
　　　聊天儿。

小雨：你怎么认识他的呢？

大海：我们两个人的学校是姐妹学
　　　校，两个学校的学生常常一
　　　起参加比赛、表演等活动。

小雨：他们的学校怎么样？课程跟
　　　你们一样吗？每天忙不忙？

大海：他们的课程跟我们一样，可
　　　是作业比我们多，所以他比
　　　我忙一些。
　　　　máng

小雨：你们有时间见面吗？

大海：当然有。下个星期两个学校就
　　　有足球比赛，我们都是队员。

小雨：在哪儿比赛？我也想去看看。

大海：就在我们学校的运动场。

小雨：我希望你们在下午比赛，
　　　因为我们上午有课。

大海：比赛下午4点才开始。
　　　　　　　　cái

小雨：太好了！我4点去看你们
　　　比赛。

大海：那天一定会很热闹！欢迎
　　　你来！

大海：我一定去。再见！
　　　　　　　zàijiàn

网络太有用了

现在我们差不多每天都用网络，你能想一下没有网络的世界会怎
wǎngluò
么样吗？我觉得网络太有用了，爸爸妈妈每天的工作都要用网络，
yǒuyòng
我每天也上网。学校的老师会在网上告诉我们最新的课程和活动。有
时候课程很难，我就用网络跟同学或者老师联系，让他们帮助我。做
ràng
作业的时候我会上网找资料。除了看电子邮件，我也常常用网络看新
huì
闻、听音乐、跟朋友聊天儿。

用网络跟人们交流很方便，也很便宜。要是我想知道我们的城市
哪里有好看的电影、比赛和表演，也总是上网查看一下。无聊的时
chákàn　　　　　wúliáo
候，我也上网玩游戏。网络上有许多免费的课程，让我有机会学一些
jīhuì
新东西。

昨天是星期五，我上网上到很晚。今天早上妈妈告诉我，"不能这
样，如果上网的时间太长，你的眼睛会不好。"我也觉得现在眼睛不太
好了。我告诉妈妈，以后每天我最多上网两个小时，但是不上网是不可
以的，因为网络对我们的生活太重要了，我们不能没有网络！
shēnghuó

Exercises

Read 1 Put a cross in the correct box according to Part I of the text.

1) Whom is Dahai talking with besides Xiaoyu?

A	B	C
Classmate	Sister	Net friend

2) How much homework does the net friend have?

A	B	C
More	Less	Same

3) What will there be next week?

A	B	C
Music show	Singing match	Football match

Listen 2 You are listening to a boy talking about an activity of a flea market. Answer the following questions in English.

1) Where will he go this Saturday?

....

2) What did he mention that he can bring?

....

3) What is this activity for according to the teacher?

....

4) Does he like this activity? Why?

....

5) Can you write down the pinyin for flea market?

....

Read 3 Put a cross to the five correct answers according to Part Ⅱ of the text.

A Sam has received the pictures Xiaohai sent him.

B I can check courses and activities online.

C I use the Internet for fun only, not for studying.

D I can learn something new online.

E My mother doesn't want me to log onto the Internet.

F There are some problems with my eyes because I spend too much time online.

G My mother permits me to use the computer for only two hours everyday.

H I cannot live without the Internet.

Talk 4 Read the following paragraph and answer the questions below in Chinese.

　　我有一个网友，她的学校和我的学校是姐妹学校。我们常常上网聊天儿，说说课程、爱好、朋友。在学校她的课程和我们的一样，不过作业多、考试多，所以她总是很忙，没有很多时间做自己喜欢的事，常常觉得学校的生活很无聊。我们的学校好一些，学生有更多的时间做自己的事。虽然考试不容易，可是我喜欢我们学校的教学（jiàoxué，teaching）方法。只有这个方法才能让我们知道我们对什么感兴趣、有什么问题、怎么学习，等等。我们学校的活动也比她们学校多，常常有比赛、表演，我也总是很忙，不过忙得很快乐。

1) What do 'we' talk about online?

....

2) How does the net friend feel about her school life? Why?

....

3) What's the difference in studying at 'my' school?

....

4) Do 'I' like the way of studying in 'my' school? Why?

....

5) What am 'I' often busy at? What do 'I' feel?

....

Our Schools Are Sister Schools 我们两个学校是姐妹学校 **11**

Talk 5

You are working with a friend to organise a Chinese talent show. You could mention:

1）The reason you are going to organise a Chinese talent show.

2）Plan for the Chinese show including time, place, etc.

3）Types of performance.

4）Schedule of practice including time, place, etc.

Write 6

Essay Plan Form

Essay title:
Write a poster to introduce the Chinese talent show.

1) The theme of the show

2) Time and venue to organize the show

3) All types of performance are welcome

4) How to contact you for more information

Your conclusion

八十五 **85**

Read 7 Reorganize the following sentences and create a short paragraph.

1）如果上网的时间太长，你的眼睛会不好。

2）昨天是星期五，我上网上到很晚。

3）我也觉得现在眼睛不太好了。

4）今天早上妈妈告诉我，不能这样。

5）我们差不多每天都在用网络。

6）我告诉妈妈，以后每天我最多上网上两个小时。

第十二课 Lesson **12**

Health Activities in the Community
社区里的健康活动

Learning Objectives

交际话题 Topic of conversation:

社区服务 Community Service
Shèqū fúwù

基本句型 Sentence patterns:

谁都不认识他。

大家可以去问专家怎么吃喝才是健康的。

我刚才见到她了。

一个人说完一句，然后下一个人说。

New Words

1 展览会 zhǎnlǎnhuì **n.** exhibition

2 大家 dàjiā **n.** everyone

3 专家 zhuānjiā **n.** expert

4 更 gèng **adv.** even more

5 刚才 gāngcái **n.** just now

6 十字路口 shízì lùkǒu **n.** crossroad

7 分别 fēnbié **adv.** seperately

8 比如 bǐrú **v.** such as

9 继续 jìxù **v.** to go on; to continue

10 回答 huídá **v./n.** to answer; answer

11 句 jù **n.** sentence

12 下一个 xià yí gè next one

Text

Part I

（天天和丽丽在社区里）

天天：今天有什么事情吗？社区里为什么那么热闹？

丽丽：你不知道吗？今天社区里有一个健康活动。

天天：是吗？什么人参加？做什么呢？

丽丽：住在社区里的人们都可以参加。中心花园里有一个免费的展览会，大家可以去问
zhǎnlǎnhuì　　dàjiā
专家怎么吃喝才是健康的。
zhuānjiā
还有音乐表演、乒乓球比赛、包饺子比赛等等。

天天：太有趣了！你也打算参加吗？

丽丽：是的。我打算和妈妈参加包饺子比赛。

天天：我对乒乓球比赛更感兴趣。
gèng
我去找玛丽，请她和我一起去打乒乓球。

丽丽：我刚才见到她了，她说要去
gāngcái

看看音乐表演。

天天：为什么去看表演？打乒乓球更有意思，你觉得呢？

丽丽：我觉得两个活动都好。玛丽喜欢哪一个，我不清楚。你去问问她吧。

天天：她在哪儿？

丽丽：刚才我看见她在包饺子比赛的地方，现在我不知道她在哪儿。

天天：我去找她。包饺子比赛的地方在哪儿？

丽丽：一直往前走，到十字路口左转。
shízì　lùkǒu

天天：好，我去找她。

一个有意思的活动

大家好！欢迎大家来参加这个"认识新朋友"的活动。现在让我来告诉你们怎么做。

这里有五个新朋友，大家都不认识他们。他们分别叫"一号"、
fēnbié
"二号"、"三号"……你们每个人先想一个问题问"一号"，比如，
bǐrú
"你叫什么名字？""你喜欢什么？""你家住在哪儿？"第一个人问了以后，第二个人问，可是不能问一样的问题。大家都问了一号以后，
继续问"二号"新朋友。问"二号"朋友的问题当然可以跟问"一号"
jìxù
的一样，也可以不一样。问这些新朋友的时候，你们不能写下他们的
回答。五个新朋友都回答了以后，我叫"一号"，你们就要给我介绍
huídá
他，说说他的姓名、学校、爱好、家里有什么宠物，等等，一个人说完
一句，然后下一个人说。要是谁介绍得不对，就要给大家唱歌。要是
jù　xià yí gè
大家都说对了，就请"一号"给大家唱歌。介绍了"一号"，继续介绍
jìxù
"二号"，一直介绍到"五号"。

Exercises

Read 1 Put a cross in the correct box according to Part I of the text.

1) What is going on today in the community?

A	B	C
Sports match	Concert	Health activity

2) What is the activity that is not included?

A	B	C
Table tennis	Cooking match	Taiji show

3) Who will participate in making dumplings?

A	B	C
Tiantian and Mary	Lily and her mother	Tiantian and Lily

Listen 2 You are listening to a boy talking about an activity in the community. Answer the following questions in English.

1) What kind of people live in the community?

....

2) What is the activity for?

....

3) What can people do in this activity?

....

4) What did 'I' do?

....

5) What do 'I' think about the activity? Why?

....

Read 3

Put a cross to the five correct answers according to Part Ⅱ of the text.

A People don't know each other there.

B Everyone asked questions of the other people at the same time.

C You can give the same question to another person.

D You can not write down their answer.

E You have to introduce the new friend according to what you can remember.

F You have to sing a song if you introduce someone incorrectly.

G We can ask the person to first sing a song before we start to introduce him/her.

H You have to sing a song if you are introduced correctly by others.

Talk 4

Read the following paragraph and answer the questions below in Chinese.

　　我和小小都住在"春和"社区。我们的社区人不多，所以大家都认识。见面的时候，我们都说"你好"。要是你家里有事，别人都会来帮助。有的时候爸爸妈妈工作到很晚，我就在小小家吃饭、学习，他的爸爸妈妈对我很好。社区里有一位老人一百岁了，大家常常帮助他买东西、做饭。在重要的节日，很多人都请他到自己家里一起庆祝，可是他只能去一家。我真喜欢我们的社区。

1) How about the relation between people in the community?

....

2) Are these people friendly to others?

....

3) What do people do when someone has problems?

....

4) How do Xiaoxiao's parents provide help when 'my' parents could not take care of 'me'?

....

5) What did people do to help the old man?

....

Talk 5 You are answering your parents' questions about a visit in a gallery. You could mention:

1）There's an exhibition of Chinese modern art.

2）The organiser will give an explanation.

3）You wish the organiser to answer some of your questions.

4）What you have learnt from this exhibition.

Write 6

Essay Plan Form
Essay title:
Write a poster to introduce your Chinese class for all the parents who are coming to the open day in your school.
1) Your warm welcome
2) Interesting and practical activities in your class
3) Relation between teachers and students
4) Your classrooms' progress
Your conclusion

Read 7 Reorganize the following sentences and create a short paragraph.

1）要是谁介绍得不对，就要给大家唱歌。要是大家都说对了，就请"一号"给大家唱歌。

2）五个新朋友都回答了以后，我叫"一号"，你们就要给我介绍他。

3）介绍了"一号"，继续介绍"二号"，一直介绍到"五号"。

4）这里有五个新朋友，大家谁都不认识他们。

5）你们每个人先想一个问题问"一号"。第一个人问了以后，第二个人问，可是不能问一样的问题。

6）大家都问了"一号"以后，继续问"二号"新朋友。

北京奥运会的会标——"中国印"

北京奥运会会标将中国传统的印章和书法等艺术形式，结合起来，它形似汉字"京"，经过夸张变形，幻化成一个向前奔跑、舞动着迎接胜利的运动人形。会标既有运动的特征，体现了奥林匹克精神，又形象地表达出北京张开双臂欢迎八方宾客的热情。

Dancing Beijing: Emblem of the 2008 Summer Olympics

The official emblem of the 2008 Summer Olympics in Beijing draws on a variety of traditional Chinese cultural elements. The seal is depicted with a calligraphic rendition of the Chinese character 京 in the form of a dancing figure. The figure represents the Olympic spirit and symbolises the invitation of China opening its arms to the world.

第四单元小结	Unit Four Summary
1　要是……就…… 　　If … , ….	要是天气好，我们就去公园。 If the weather is fine, we will go to the park. 你要是有问题就问一下老师吧。 If you have any questions, ask your teacher.
2　越来越＋形容词。 　　越来越 + adjective.	我的汉语说得越来越好。 My oral Chinese is getting better. 天气越来越热。 The weather is getting warmer.
3　动词词组＋差不多＋要＋时间词。 　　Verb phrase + 差不多 + 要 + time noun.	骑自行车差不多要半个小时。 It took almost half an hour by bike. 走到学校差不多要20分钟。 It took about 20 minutes to walk to school.
4　某人₁/某物＋让＋某人₂＋动词词组。 　　Sb.₁/sth. + 让 + sb.₂ + verb phrase.	我让哥哥帮助我。 I asked my elder brother to help me. 网络课程让我学习了很多新东西。 Online courses taught me many new things.
5　某人/某事物＋时间词＋才＋动词词组。 　　Sb./sth. + time noun + 才 + verb phrase.	他花了一个小时才做好作业。 It took him an hour to finish his homework. 比赛4点才开始。 The match will not begin until four.
6　除了……以外，也…… 　　Besides …, ….	除了看电子邮件以外，我也常常在网络上跟朋友聊天。 Besides checking for emails, I always chat online with my friends. 除了老人以外，也有一些工作的年轻人晚上到广场散步。 Besides seniors, some young men will go walking in the square after work.

第四单元小结	Unit Four Summary
7 **某人＋不怎么＋……** Sb. + 不怎么 + ….	我不怎么清楚。 I'm not so sure. 姐姐不怎么喜欢那个工作。 My sister doesn't like that job very much.
8 **A＋比＋B＋更＋形容词。** A + compare + B + 更 + adjective.	这个社区比那个更大。 This community is bigger than that one. 地铁比公共汽车汽车更方便。 The subway is more convenient than the bus.
9 **谁＋都＋动词＋…** 谁 + 都 + verb +….	谁都知道这个展览会。 Everybody knew of this exhibition. 谁都不认识他。 Nobody knew him.

第十三课 Lesson 13

I Am His Fan
我是他的粉丝

Learning Objectives

交际话题 Topic of conversation:

社会名人 Celebrities
Shèhuì míngrén

基本句型 Sentence patterns:

他是来接林书豪的。

我们正说他呢，他就来了。

他有很多粉丝。

New Words

1. 接 jiē **v.** to pick up
2. 林书豪 Lín Shūháo Jeremy Lin, a famous basketball player
3. 姚明 Yáo Míng Yao Ming, a famous Chinese basketball player
4. 粉丝 fěnsī **n.** fan
5. 队 duì **n.** team
6. (颜)色 (yán)sè **n.** colour
7. 运动服 yùndòngfú **n.** sportswear
8. 白 bái **adj.** white
9. 蓝 lán **adj.** blue
10. 明星 míngxīng **n.** star
11. 纽约 Niǔyuē **n.** New York City
12. 遇到 yùdào **v.** to come across
13. 华人 huárén **n.** Chinese people
14. 当天 dàngtiān that very day

Text

Part I

（玛丽、大卫在机场）

玛丽：大卫，你好！你要去旅行吗？

大卫：不，我是来接林书豪的。
jiē Lín Shūháo

玛丽：林书豪是谁？

大卫：他是美国的篮球运动员。
今天他从纽约来北京。
Niǔyuē

玛丽：篮球运动员我只知道姚明。
Yáo Míng

大卫：我觉得林书豪现在比姚明
有名。

玛丽：这么多人都是来接他的吗？

大卫：我们都是来接他的。

玛丽：你是他的粉丝吗？
fěnsī

大卫：当然。在中国，他已经有很
多粉丝了。

玛丽：我不常看体育新闻，第一次
听说他的名字。

大卫：我喜欢看体育节目，现在

特别喜欢看林书豪打篮球。
我还参加了我们学校的篮球
队，我差不多天天下午打篮球。
duì

玛丽：你知道他穿的运动服是什么
yùndòngfú
颜色的吗？
yánsè

大卫：当然知道。他现在穿红色7号
球衣，以前穿蓝色和白色球衣。
lán   bái

玛丽：哈哈，你真的是他的粉丝！

大卫：玛丽，你来机场接人吗？

玛丽：是的。我来接我的朋友，她从
纽约来。

我是他的粉丝

今天下午林书豪要来我们学校参观。同学们听到这个新闻，都很高兴，因为我们都是他的粉丝。他现在是美国有名的篮球运动员。他先看我们学校的篮球比赛。比赛后，林书豪给我们表演打篮球。

在我们篮球队的休息室里，有许多篮球运动员的照片，当然也有林书豪的。下午比赛的时候，我们队穿跟他一样的红色运动服。在中国，林书豪现在有很多粉丝，我想因为他是华人吧。昨天下午他是坐飞机来的，我和粉丝们去了机场接他。很多记者也在机场等他，有报纸杂志的记者，也有电视记者。我还遇到了我的朋友玛丽。我们正说他呢，他就来了。当天晚上的电视节目里，我们就看到了他来中国的新闻，我还看见了玛丽和我自己。这也是我第一次在电视上看到自己。

Exercises

Read 1 Put a cross in the correct box according to Part I of the text.

1) Where do David and Mary meet?

A	B	C
Railway station	Airport	Police station

2) Whom will David pick up?

A	B	C
A famous basketball player	A Chinese movie star	A friend from New York

3) What is David doing here?

A	B	C
To meet a basketball star	To pick up a friend	To see David

Listen 2 You are listening to an introduction of Yao Ming. Answer the following questions in English.

1) What's sport does Yao Ming play?

....

2) Where are Yao Ming's fans from?

....

3) Which part of China is Yao Ming from?

....

4) Where did Yao Ming play basketball when he was 22 years old?

....

5) How old was Yao Ming when he came back to Shanghai?

....

Read 3
Put a cross to the five correct answers according to Part II of the text.

A Jeremy Lin is coming to visit our school this afternoon.

B Jeremy Lin will watch us play basketball in China.

C I am Jeremy's fan.

D There are some movie stars' posters in the room of our basketball team.

E We are going to wear red jerseys this afternoon.

F Jeremy Lin has many fans in China.

G Jeremy Lin arrived in Beijing by air yesterday.

H There were TV show stars in the airport yesterday afternoon.

Talk 4
Read the following paragraph and answer the questions below in Chinese.

　　我常看唱歌、跳舞比赛的节目，很多参加比赛的人很快成为（chéngwéi, to become）了明星。我也很喜欢唱歌，想去参加电视唱歌比赛，让更多的人听我唱歌。每天下课后我都练习唱歌。我的老师以前就是有名的歌星。我父母都是他的粉丝，他们会唱很多我老师的歌，这些歌都很好听。我想跟我的老师一样，唱自己写的歌，唱给更多的人听。每年学校有圣诞晚会的时候，我都表演唱歌，学校的同学们说我唱得像明星一样好。

1) Why do 'I' like watching song and dance TV competitions?

....

2) What do 'I' do after school everyday?

....

3) Who is 'my' singing teacher?

....

4) Who is 'my' parents' idol?

....

5) What did 'I' do in the annual Christmas party for our school?

....

Talk 5 You are going to introduce a famous person to your classmates. You will talk about:

1) The country where the person is from. 2) The occupation of the person.

3) The success of the person. 4) His favourite colour.

5) The reason you choose the person.

Write 6

Essay Plan Form

Essay title:

You are going to interview a famous person. Write an interview outline.

1) Interview purpose

2) A brief introduction of the person

3) The question you are planning to ask

4) The person's next plan for his/her career

5) Your wishes and blessings for the person

Your conclusion

Read 7

Reorganize the following sentences and create a short paragraph.

1）他现在是有名的篮球运动员。

2）下午比赛的时候，我们队都穿跟他一样的红色运动服。

3）今天下午林书豪来我们学校参观。

4）他先看我们学校的篮球比赛。比赛后，林书豪给我们表演打篮球。

5）同学们听到这个新闻，都很高兴，因为我们都是他的粉丝。

第十四课 Lesson 14

Knowledge of History Helps to Understand the Future
不知道历史，就不知道将来

Learning Objectives

交际话题 Topic of conversation:

中外 历史 名人 Famous People in China
Zhōng-wài lìshǐ míngrén and Foreign Countries

基本句型 Sentence patterns:

李白和杜甫都是古代有名的诗人。
他们跟莎士比亚一样重要。
中国人过端午节纪念屈原。

New Words

1 名人 míngrén n. celebrity
2 屈原 Qū Yuán Qu Yuan, an ancient Chinese poet
3 龙舟 lóngzhōu n. dragon boat
4 纪念 jìniàn v. to remember
5 李白 Lǐ Bái Li Bai, an ancient Chinese poet
6 杜甫 Dù Fǔ Du Fu, an ancient Chinese poet
7 诗人 Shīrén n. poet

8 莎士比亚 Shāshìbǐyà William Shakespeare
9 百 bǎi num. hundred
10 文学 wénxué n. literature
11 赵氏孤儿 Zhàoshì Gū'ér Orphan of the Zhao Family, a Chiese Drama
12 千 qiān num. thousand
13 农历 nónglì n. the traditional Chinese calendar
14 作品 zuòpǐng n. works

Text

| Part I |

小雨：本，你好！你来图书馆读书吗？

本：　是。我来找几本中国历史的书。

小雨：你对中国历史有兴趣吗？

本：　是的。我打算学习中国历史，准备先读一些书。

小雨：中国的历史很长，你知道什么历史故事或者历史名人吗？
　　　　　　　　　　　　　　　　　　　　　　　　　míngrén

本：　我知道屈原。每年农历五月的时候，中国人过端午节纪念屈
　　　Qū Yuán　　　nónglì wǔ yuè　　　　　　　　　　jìniàn
　　　原，还要赛龙舟、吃粽子。
　　　　　　　lóngzhōu

小雨：你说得很对！

本：　因为我喜欢历史，所以读过一些中国的故事。我还知道李白
　　　　　　　　　　　　　　　　　　　　　　　　　　　Lǐ Bái
　　　和杜甫，他们都是古代有名的诗人。
　　　　Dù Fǔ　　　　　　　　　　shīrén

小雨：他们在中国历史上很重要。差不
　　　多每个中国人都知道他们。

本：　我知道，他们跟英国的莎士比亚
　　　　　　　　　　　　　　Shāshìbǐyà
　　　一样重要。

小雨：对，我就很喜欢读莎士比亚的书。

本：　英国的小学生都知道莎士比亚，
　　　中学生都要读他的书。

小雨：莎士比亚在中国也很有名，很多
　　　中学生在文学课上都学过莎士比亚
　　　　　　　wénxué
　　　的作品。
　　　　zuòpǐn

本： 莎士比亚三百多年前写的故事，我们现在读还觉得很有意思。
bǎi

小雨： 故事虽然有意思，可是用英语读，我觉得非常难懂。

本： 我也觉得很难。因为他是用古代的英语写的，现在的人们都不用了。

小雨： 本，你喜欢中国历史，我喜欢英国文学，那以后我们一起学习怎么样？

本： 太好了，我们一起努力。

Part II

不知道历史，就不知道将来

我是一名学习汉语的大学生，来自英国。我的中国朋友问我为什么学汉语，为什么来中国。我告诉他们，我喜欢历史，打算学习中国历史。如果我要学习中国历史，当然要先学习汉语，还要学习古代汉语。

中国的历史很长，有很多有意思的故事，也有很多历史名人。《赵氏孤儿》是两千多年前的故事，我现在读还是觉得很有意思。很多欧洲
qiān

人也知道这个有名的中国故事。不过我读的是英文的，我希望有一天我能用中文读这个故事。如果你问我为什么喜欢历史，我觉得每个人都应该学习一点儿历史，因为不知道历史，就不知道将来。年轻人应该多读历史书。

Exercises

 Read 1 Put a cross in the correct box according to Part I of the text.

1) What kind of books does Ben find in library?

A	B	C
English history	Chinese literature	Chinese history

2) Which festival is celebrated in China in the fifth month of the Chinese calender?

A	B	C
The Dragon Boat Festival	The Spring Festival	The Lantern Festival

3) What does Xiaoyu plan to study?

A	B	C
Chinese literature	Chinese ancient poetry	English literature

Listen 2 You are listening to an introduction of Wang Xiaoli. Answer the following questions in English.

1) How long has Wang Xiaoli studied English?

....

2) What kind of materials did Wang Xiaoli's English teacher use in English class?

....

3) What kind of books did Wang Xiaoli read?

....

4) What kind of books would Wang Xiaoli like to read?

....

5) What's Wang Xiaoli's plan when she graduates from high school?

....

Read
3

Put a cross to the five correct answers according to Part II of the text.

A He is a student from Britain.

B He came to China to learn Chinese literature.

C He plans to study Chinese history.

D He also wants to learn ancient Chinese language.

E The story *Orphan of the Zhao Family* was from two thousand years ago.

F Many Europeans know the story *Orphan of the Zhao Family*.

G He reads the story in Chinese.

H He studies Chinese poems in order to learn Chinese history.

Talk
4

Read the following paragraph and answer the questions below in Chinese.

　　我家旁边的城市广场上有一个中国艺术展览会，周末我和我的中国朋友小红去参观了。我买了几个中国历史电影的 DVD。中国的历史很长，有很多有意思的故事，也有很多历史名人。因为我喜欢中国历史，所以看过一些中国的历史电影。有一个是香港电影《屈原》，我非常喜欢。看了那个电影后，我知道了中国人过端午节是为了（wèile，for）纪念屈原。在端午节的时候吃粽子、赛龙舟也都跟纪念屈原有关系（yǒu guānxì，to be related）。我在展览会上也买了这个电影的 DVD，我还要再看一遍（yí biàn，once）。

1) Where was the Chinese Art exhibition?

....

2) Who went with 'me'?

....

3) What did 'I' buy in the exhibition?

....

4) Why did 'I' see some Chinese movies?

....

5) Why do Chinese people celebrate the Dragon Boat Festival?

....

Talk 5

You are going to introduce a famous historical figure to your classmates. You will talk about:

1) The social background of his/her time.

2) This person's stories.

3) His/her works.

4) What you have learnt from him/her.

Write 6

Essay Plan Form

Essay title:

You are going to prepare a presentation to introduce Qu Yuan. Write a PowerPoint outline.

1) The social background of his time

2) His poetic works

3) The origin of Dragon Boat Festival

4) Zongzi (rice dumpling)

5) The way Chinese people celebrate Dragon Boat Festival nowadays

Your conclusion

Read 7 Reorganize the following sentences and create a short paragraph.

1）如果我要学习中国历史，当然要先学习汉语，还要学习古代汉语。

2）不过我读的是英文的，我希望有一天我能用中文读这个故事。

3）我是一名学习汉语的大学生，我来自英国。

4）中国的历史很长，有很多有意思的故事，也有很多历史名人。《赵氏孤儿》是两千多年前的故事，我现在读还是觉得很有意思。

5）我的中国朋友问我为什么学汉语，为什么来中国。我告诉他们，我喜欢历史，打算学习中国历史。

6）很多欧洲人也知道这个有名的中国故事。

第十五课 Lesson

15

Reading and Travelling Are Both Important
读书和旅行都重要

Learning Objectives

交际话题 Topic of conversation:

服装与时尚：Clothing and Fashion
Fúzhuāng yǔ shíshàng

基本句型 Sentence patterns:

你跟我一起去买东西吧？
如果在商场买不到，我想在书店
应该买得到。
我会拍许多照片，用电子邮件发
给他们。

New Words

1. 商场 shāngchǎng **n.** shopping mall
2. 书店 shūdiàn **n.** bookstore
3. T恤 T-xù **n.** T-shirt
4. 短 duǎn **adj.** short
5. 裙子 qúnzi **n.** skirt
6. 裤子 kùzi **n.** trousers
7. 鞋 xié **n.** shoes
8. 文化 wénhuà **n.** culture
9. 照相机 zhàoxiàngjī **n.** camera
10. 雨伞 yǔsǎn **n.** umbrella
11. 件 jiàn **m.w.** (a measure word used for clothing)
12. 毛衣 máoyī **n.** sweater

Text

Part I

（玛丽和小雨边走路边聊天儿）

玛丽：这个周末你有时间吗？

小雨：有时间。你打算做什么？

玛丽：你跟我一起去买东西吧？

小雨：好的。你要买什么东西？

玛丽：我想买几张欧洲古典音乐的CD，在哪儿能买到？

小雨：如果在商场买不到，我想在
书店应该买得到。
shūdiàn

玛丽：我正想去书店呢。我打算放假去欧洲旅行，想买几本介绍欧洲的书看看。

小雨：行，我也喜欢去书店，我每次去都看很长时间的书。除了书和CD，你还买什么？

玛丽：我还想买旅行时穿的衣服。

小雨：你打算放暑假去吗？

玛丽：对，我打算八月去。

小雨：那T恤、短的裙子和裤子都要
T-xù duǎn qúnzi kùzi
准备一些。

玛丽：好的。大海要去参加篮球比赛，让我替他买运动服和运动鞋。
xié

小雨：他喜欢什么颜色的？

玛丽：白色或者蓝色的吧，我常常看见他穿这两个颜色的衣服。

读书和旅行一样重要

我学习英语五年了，可是我还没去过英语国家。爸爸妈妈说，今年暑假让我去英国旅行。我可以住在爸爸的朋友家。我高兴极了！

我从现在就开始准备了。周末，我准备去买几本介绍英国的书，还想买几本莎士比亚的书和几张英国的音乐CD。我可以在飞机上一边听音乐一边看书。如果我去一个地方旅行，我一定要读一些那里的历史和文化书。wénhuà因为我觉得读书和旅行一样重要。爸爸妈妈送给我一个新的照相机。zhàoxiàngjī我会拍许多照片，用电子邮件发给他们，告诉他们我去过的地方和看到的人。旅行的书上说，英国常常下雨，雨伞yǔsǎn一定要准备。下雨的时候有点儿冷，我应该多准备几件衣服。有的朋友告诉我，英国的北边比南边冷，要准备一件毛衣。jiàn máoyī如果不去旅行，我还不知道英国的夏天要穿毛衣呢。

Exercises

Read 1 Put a cross in the correct box according to Part I of the text.

1) What does Mary ask Xiaoyu to do this weekend?

A	B	C
Go running	Go mountain climbing	Go shopping

2) Where can Mary buy European music CDs?

A	B	C
In a bookstore	In a supermarket	In a market

3) What does Dahai ask Mary to help him buy?

A	B	C
Music CDs and books	Skirt and trousers	Sport clothing and shoes

Listen 2 You are listening to a shopping plan. Answer the following questions in English.

1) Where do I plan to travel to?

....

2) What do I want to buy for the trip?

....

3) What do I want to buy for my parents' friends?

....

4) What am I going to buy for David?

....

5) What is David's favourite colour?

....

Read
3

Put a cross to the five correct answers according to Part II of the text.

A I have studied English for five years.

B I have been to the UK once.

C My parents send me to the UK for travelling.

D I have started preparing for the trip this week.

E I have bought some books and sports shoes for myself.

F If I travel somewhere, I should study some of the history of that place in advance.

G In my opinion, reading is more important than travelling.

H My parents gave me a camera.

Talk
4

Read the following paragraph and answer the questions below in Chinese.

　　因为我喜欢拍照片，爸爸、妈妈在去年送给我一个数码（shùmǎ, digital）照相机，那是给我的生日礼物，以后我看演唱会、参观博物馆、去公园、旅行、买东西、去餐厅吃饭的时候，我都会拍几张照片。我看到漂亮的东西就想拍，现在已经拍了一万（yī wàn, ten thousand）张照片了。今年暑假我要去欧洲旅行，我看介绍欧洲的书上说，欧洲非常漂亮，我可以照很多照片。数码照相机很方便，每天都可以用电子邮件发给北京的朋友们，让他们看到我去过的地方和见过的人。

1) What birthday gift did 'my' parents give 'me' last year?

....

2) What is 'my' hobby?

....

3) On what occasion do 'I' usually take photographs?

....

4) Where should 'I' travel to during this summer vacation?

....

5) Why do 'I' send the digital photos to 'my' friends in Beijing?

....

Talk 5

You are going to show your friends where they can buy the things they need. You will talk about:

1）Food, like milk, bread, juice, tea, fruits.

2）Clothes, like sweater, skirt, trousers.

3）Books and music CDs.

4）TV set, fridge, camera.

5）What you don't want to buy.

Write 6

Essay Plan Form
Essay title: You are going to travel for 2 weeks. Write a list for packing.
1) Travel certificates
2) Funds
3) Things for meals and accommodation
4) Things for sightseeing
5) Things for communication
Your conclusion

Read
7
Reorganize the following sentences and create a short paragraph.

1）如果我去什么地方旅行，我一定要读一些那里的历史和文化书。

2）今年暑假我要去英国旅行。

3）我从现在开始准备去英国的旅行。

4）因为我觉得读书和旅行一样重要。

5）我可以在飞机上一边听音乐一边看书。

6）周末，我准备去买几本介绍英国的书，还想买几本莎士比亚的书和几张英国音乐的CD。

诗人李白

　　李白（701—762），字太白，号青莲居士。中国唐朝最杰出的诗人，被誉为"诗仙"，李白也是中国文学史上继屈原之后又一位伟大的浪漫主义诗人。他与同时代的现实主义诗人杜甫并称"李杜"。李白流传下来的诗文有上千篇，代表作有《静夜思》、《早发白帝城》、《蜀道难》、《将进酒》等。

Li Bai

Li Bai (701-762), whose courtesy name was Taibai and literary name Qinglian Jushi, was one of the greatest poets of the Tang Dynasty and honoured as the "Poet Transcendent". Similar to Qu Yuan, Li Bai was noted for his romantic writing style. Li Bai, and the other great poet of his time, Du Fu, were together called "Li Du"; they had achieved the heights of the poetic arts in the Tang Dynasty. Around a thousand extant poems are attributed by him, such as: *A Quiet Night Thought*, *Leaving White King City at Dawn*, *The Hard Road*, and *Bringing in the Wine*.

第五单元小结　Unit Five Summary

1　某人＋从＋某地₁＋来／去＋某地₂。 Sb. + 从 + somewhere₁ + 来 / 去 + somewhere₂.	我从家里去。 I will go from home. 她从纽约来北京。 She came to Beijing from New York.
2　某人＋是＋补充词组。 Sb. + 是 + complementary phrase.	他是坐飞机来的。 He flew here. 我是在网上学的。 I learnt it from the Internet.
3　某人₁＋正＋动词词组₁＋呢（助词），某人₂＋就＋动词词组₂。 Sb.₁ + 正 + verb phrase₁ + particle word 呢 , sb.₂ + 就 + verb phrase₂.	我们正说他呢，他就来了。 He got here when we were talking about him. 妈妈正做饭呢，爸爸就回家了。 Dad got home when Mum was cooking.
4　某人＋在历史上＋形容词。 Sb. + 在历史上 + adjective.	莎士比亚在英国历史上很重要。 Shakespeare plays a very important role in English history. 他们在历史上很有名。 They are very famous in history.
5　因为……，所以…… Because ..., ...	因为学校不远，所以我走路去。 I walk to school because it is close. 因为我喜欢历史，所以我看了很多历史书。 I read a lot of historical books because I like history.
6　某人₁＋某人₂＋都＋动词＋名词／动词词组。 Sb.₁ + sb.₂ + 都 + verb+ noun/verb phrase.	小明和小英都喜欢看书。 Both Xiaoming and Xiaoying enjoy reading books. 李白和杜甫都是有名的诗人。 Both Li Bai and Du Fu are famous poets.

第五单元小结 Unit Five Summary

7	动词＋得／不＋到。 Verb + 得／不 + 到.	买得到/买不到 You can/can't buy it. 看得到(见)/看不到(见) You can/can't see it.
8	某人＋动词＋到＋了（＋名词）。 Sb. + verb + 到了 (+ noun).	他听到了。 He heard you. 我吃到了月饼。 I ate some moon cakes.

第十六课 Lesson

16

The Underground Station Is Quite Close from Here
地铁站离这儿很近

Learning Objectives

交际话题 Topic of conversation:

旅游信息和服务
Lǚyóu xìnxī hé fúwù
Travel Information and Services

基本句型 Sentence patterns:

火车站离这儿多远?

地铁站离这儿很近。

地铁票贵不贵?

这里的特产是什么?

New Words

1. 路人 lùrén **n.** passerby
2. 酒店 jiǔdiàn **n.** hotel
3. 前台 qiántái **n.** information and reception counter
4. 信用卡 xìnyòngkǎ **n.** credit card
5. 护照 hùzhào **n.** passport
6. 特产 tèchǎn **n.** local specialty
7. 风筝 fēngzheng **n.** kite
8. 行李 xíngli **n.** luggage
9. 空调 kōngtiáo **n.** air-conditioning
10. 饭 fàn **n.** meal
11. 点菜 diǎn cài **v.** to order dishes
12. 付钱 fù qián **v.** to pay
13. 太阳 tàiyáng **n.** sun

Text

Part I

（在路边，大卫在问一个路人）
路人 lùrén

大卫：你好！我要去火车站。请问，火车站离这儿远吗？

路人：火车站离这儿很远，你坐公共汽车去吧。

大卫：坐地铁能到吗？

路人：坐地铁也能到。

大卫：请问，地铁站在哪儿？

路人：地铁站离这儿很近。往前走，你就看到了。

大卫：地铁票贵不贵？

路人：不贵，很便宜，每个人两块钱。

大卫：谢谢您。

（在酒店前台）
酒店 前台 jiǔdiàn qiántái

大卫：你好！

服务员：您好，先生！

大卫：请问，有房间吗？

服务员：有。我们有大房间，也有小房间。

大卫：我要小房间。

服务员：你要住几天？

大卫：我打算住两天。我可以用信用卡付钱吗？
信用卡 付钱 xìnyòngkǎ fù qián

服务员：当然可以。

大卫：那太好了。

服务员：先生，我能看看您的护照吗？
护照 hùzhào

大卫：这是我的护照。

服务员：给。您的行李多吗？我帮您叫服务员吧？
行李 xíngli

大卫：我的行李不多，我自己可以。请问这里的特产是什么？
特产 tèchǎn

服务员：我们这个地方的风筝很有名。
风筝 fēngzheng

大卫：我要买几个送给我的朋友们。

我喜欢这个小城市

上周末我去了中国南方的一个小城市。它虽然很小，但是风景很漂亮，那里的人也很好。那里没有地铁，也没有公共汽车，大家都骑自行车，非常方便。

我住的酒店很干净。虽然现在是夏天，但是房间里一点儿都不热，不用开空调。在酒店吃饭，我用中文点菜。付钱的时候，服务员说我的中文很好。酒店离海边很近，我散步五分钟就到了。我在那里住了五天，每天都到海边走走，很舒服。

在海边，我看见一些年轻人在放风筝。那天天气很好，风筝在太阳下非常漂亮。我非常喜欢这个小城市，在这里我不上网，不看电视，不用手机，都不觉得无聊。我有一点儿不想回大城市了。

Exercises

Read
1
Put a cross in the correct box according to Part I of the text.

1) Where does David want to go?

A	B	C
To the bus station	To the railway station	To the underground station

2) What kind of room would David like to stay in?

A	B	C
Small room	Big room	Single room

3) How many days does David plan to stay?

A	B	C
One day	Two days	Three days

4) What does David plan to buy for his friends?

A	B	C
Books	Kites	Foods

Listen
2
You are listening to a travel diary. Answer the following questions in English.

1) Where did 'I' go with my family during the Christmas holiday?

....

2) How was the weather there?

....

3) What were the usual activities for 'my' sister and 'I'?

....

4) How far was 'my' hotel from the seaside?

....

5) What kind of sports did 'my' father do every morning?

....

6) What kind of dishes did 'we' order for lunch in the small restaurant downtown?

....

Read 3 Put a cross to the five correct answers according to Part Ⅱ of the text.

A I went to a small city during the weekend.

B There is no underground in the city.

C There is a bus system in the city.

D I stayed in a new hotel.

E The hotel is very close to the seaside.

F It's not hot at all in the room.

G I couldn't order with a Chinese menu in the restaurant.

H I didn't use the Internet, or watch TV when I was in the small city.

Talk 4 Read the following paragraph and answer the questions below in Chinese.

在好天气的时候去旅行，你就能玩得很好。参观、爬山、游泳都很方便。可是去年寒假我去了北方（běifāng，north），那里每天都下雪。除了滑雪，我们没有办法去别的地方。在我们住的酒店旁边只有一个电影院，电影院离酒店很近，我们散步就能到了。电影票不贵，我和妹妹天天去看，可是买电影票不能用信用卡，有点儿不方便。有的电影我们看不懂，所以我觉得很无聊。

1) How was the weather where 'I' visited last winter?

....

2) What were 'our' outdoor activities there?

....

3) Was the cinema far away from 'our' hotel?

....

4) How did 'we' get to the cinema?

....

5) Was the movie ticket expensive?

....

6) Did the box office accept credit card?

....

Talk 5

Your friend is coming to your city for a visit by train. You have booked a hotel for him. Please tell your friend how to come to the hotel from the train station and how to check in.

1) Directions from the railway station to the underground station.

2) Take the underground.

3) Directions from the underground station to the bus station.

4) Take the bus to the hotel.

5) Check in with passport, credit card or traveller's cheques.

6) Make a travel budget and memo for your weekend trip.

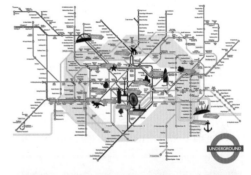

Write 6

Essay Plan Form

Essay title:

You want to help your parents decide which country they should visit. Write a note to compare the two countries.

1) Transportation expenses

2) Cost of accommodation

3) Cost of meals

4) Places of historic interest and scenic beauty

5) Local specialties

6) Travel certificates

7) Money exchange

Your conclusion

Read 7

Reorganize the following sentences and create a short paragraph.

1）小城市的风景很漂亮，那里的人也很好。

2）那天天气很好，风筝在太阳下非常漂亮。

3）在海边，我看见一些年轻人在放风筝。

4）我住的酒店离海很近。

5）我在那里住了五天，每天都在海边走走。

6）上周末我去了中国南方的一个小城市。

第十七课 Lesson **17**

Where Are You From?
你从哪里来？

Learning Objectives

交际话题 Topic of conversation:
解决问题 To Solve a Problem
Jiějué　wèntí

基本句型 Sentence patterns:
你从哪里来？
我要在这里换地铁回家。
从北京到上海坐火车要多长时间？
你坐的火车几点开？
我从日本坐飞机回国。

New Words

1 换 huàn **v.** to change, to exchange

2 日本 Rìběn **n.** Japan

3 回国 huí guó　to return to sb's mother country

4 全家 quánjiā　the whole family

5 意大利 Yìdàlì **n.** Italy

6 停车场 tíngchēchǎng **n.** parking lot

7 成人 chéngrén **n.** adult

8 解决 jiějué **v.** to solve

9 问题 wèntí **n.** question, problem

Text

Part I

（小雨在地铁站见到了大海）

小雨：大海，很久不见。你从哪里来？

大海：我刚从机场来的。在这里换地铁回家。
　　　　 huàn

小雨：你去旅行了？

大海：是的，我去外国旅行了。

小雨：你去哪个国家旅行了？

大海：我先去了英国，再从伦敦坐火车去法国。

小雨：从北京到伦敦坐飞机贵吗？

大海：不贵，因为我很早就订了学生票。你呢，要去哪里？

小雨：我要坐火车去上海，再从上海去香港。

大海：你也坐火车去香港吗？

小雨：不，我坐飞机去香港。

大海：从北京到上海坐火车要多长时间？

小雨：六个小时，坐火车很快，也很方便。

大海：你从香港还去别的地方吗？

小雨：我从香港去台湾，然后去日本，再从日本坐飞机回国。
　　　　　　Rìběn
　　　huí guó

大海：我还没去过台湾。听说那里很漂亮，很好玩儿。

小雨：我以前也没去过台湾。

大海：你的火车几点开？

小雨：三点，还有一个半小时。

大海：好，祝你玩得高兴！

Part II

开车旅行

今年暑假，我们全家开车去欧洲旅行了。我们先从伦敦坐火车到
　　　　　quánjiā
法国，再从法国开车到德国和意大利。
　　　　　　　　　　　　　　Yìdàlì

一路上我们参观了很多漂亮的小城市。有的小城市在河边，有的
在海边。在欧洲开车旅行很方便，路很好，停车场也很多。有的停
　　　　　　　　　　　　　　　　　tíngchēchǎng
车场旁边有可爱的小餐厅。我们觉得饿了、累了的时候，就去餐厅一
边吃饭一边休息。餐厅的饭很好吃，我喜欢吃德国的猪肉，也喜欢吃
法国的海鲜和意大利的面条。德国、法国和意大利的红酒都很有名，
妈妈有时喝一点酒。爸爸和哥哥开车，他们不能喝酒。我不是成人，
　　　　　　　　　　　　　　　　　　　　　　　　　　chéngrén
也不能喝酒。我们用英语点菜，服务员能听懂，但是他们说德语和法
语，我们听不懂。

开车旅行也有不好玩的时候。有一次我们的汽车在路上坏了，爸
爸给汽车公司打电话，请他们帮助我们。可是他们花了四个小时才
解决了问题。那时候，天已经黑了。
jiějué　　wèntí

Exercises

Read 1 Put a cross in the correct box according to Part I of the text.

1) Where did Dahai come from?

A	B	C
Underground station	Bus station	Airport

2) Which countries did Dahai visit?

A	B	C
UK & France	China & Germany	Germany & France

3) What was Dahai's first destination?

A	B	C
Beijing	London	Paris

4) Where did Xiaoyu come from?

A	B	C
Home	Shanghai	Hong Kong

5) Where does Xiaoyu plan to go from Hong Kong?

A	B	C
Taiwan & Japan	Shanghai & Taiwan	Beijing

Listen
2

Listen to Xiaoyu and answer the following questions in English.

1) When did Xiaoyu start off from Beijing?

....

2) What was Xiaoyu's first destination?

....

3) How long did Xiaoyu stay in the first destination?

....

4) How was the weather in Taiwan when Xiaoyu was there?

....

5) What happend to Xiaoyu when she was in Taiwan?

....

6) Who took care of Xiaoyu?

....

Read
3

Put a cross to the five correct answers according to Part II of the text.

A My whole family travelled in Europe by car this summer.

B We drove from France to Germany.

C It's very convenient to travel by car in Europe.

D My parents drank wine sometime.

E I am not an adult yet and may not drink.

F We ordered in French and German.

G The waiters and waitresses understood English.

H Our car broke down on the road, but the car rental company sent us a new car.

Talk
4

Read the following paragraph and answer the questions below in Chinese.

　　旅行让人快乐，可是也会有不快乐的时候。去年我去滑雪时，遇到了很多问题。到了那里以后，我就感冒了，咳嗽、头疼。我的家人送我去医院，那里的医院不能用信用卡。我们没有很多现金（xiànjīn, cash），爸爸给我们的朋友打电话，他们给了我们很大的帮助。我吃了医生给我的药，很快就好了。如果我的病好不了，我们就得换飞机票回家。妈妈说，以后旅行的时候要准备一点药。

1) What happened when 'I' travelled with 'my' family last winter?

....

2) What kind of problem did 'we' have in the hospital?

....

3) What did 'my' father do to figure out the problem?

....

4) Who finally helped 'us'?

....

5) If 'I' couldn't recover soon, what should 'we' do about our travel schedule?

....

6) What did 'my' mother say if 'we' are ill for a trip in the future?

....

Talk 5

You are going to help your foreign friend to call the police as he lost his important documents when he was taking a sightseeing tour in your city. Please describe some clues:

1）When he left the hotel.   2）He took the underground to go somewhere.

3）Had a sightseeing tour.   4）Had lunch in a restaurant.

5）Bought local specialty.

Write 6

Essay Plan Form

Essay title:
Make a memo in case anything unexpected happens during the journey.

1) What if you become ill

2) What if you are lost

3) What if you lose your travel certificate

4) What if your money is stolen

5) What if you can't understand the local language

6) What if you have a misunderstanding because of cross cultural communication differences

Your conclusion

Read 7 Reorganize the following sentences and create a short paragraph.

1）一路上我们参观了很多漂亮的小城市。

2）今年暑假，我们全家开车去欧洲旅行了。

3）有的小城市在河边，有的在海边，我都很喜欢。

4）有的停车场旁边有可爱的小餐厅。

5）我们觉得饿了、累了的时候，就去餐厅一边吃饭一边休息。

6）在欧洲开车旅行很方便，路很好，停车场也很多。

第十八课 Lesson 18

Sometimes Advertisements Are Very Helpful
有时候广告很有用

Learning Objectives

交际话题 Topic of conversation:

广告与商品：Advertisement and Products
Guǎnggào yǔ shāngpǐn

基本句型 Sentence patterns:

广告帮助我们了解商品的最新信息。

便宜的东西也有，贵的东西也有。

每一张照片都跟杂志上的一样好看。

New Words

1　商店 shāngdiàn **n.** shop, store

2　卖 mài **v.** to sell

3　了解 liǎojiě **v.** to know

4　打折 dǎ zhé **v.** to have a discount

5　价钱 jiàqián **n.** price

6　块 kuài **m.w.** (a measure word used for watches)

7　送 sòng **v.** to send

8　手表 shǒubiǎo **n.** watch; wrist watch

9　信息 xìnxī **n.** information

10　冰箱 bīngxiāng **n.** refrigerator

11　数码 shùmǎ **n.** digital

Text

Part I

（天天和本在聊天儿）

本：　天天，你给我介绍几个网上商店吧。
shāngdiàn

天天：你想买什么？

本：　我想买一辆自行车。我的自行车坏了。广告上说，网上商店里有最新商品，卖得也便宜。
mài

天天：是。广告帮助我们了解商品的最新信息，还能帮助我们找到便宜的商品。
liǎojiě　xìnxī

本：　很多人都是看了广告以后去买东西。

天天：虽然我们不喜欢广告，但是有时候广告很有用。

本：　你常常上网，一定知道哪个商店便宜。

天天：好，我下课以后上网找找，发邮件告诉你。

本：　谢谢你！

天天：我哥哥上星期买了一个数码
shùmǎ

照相机非常好，也很便宜。

本：　他是在网上商店买的吗？

天天：不是，他是在市中心的商场买的。

本：　比网上贵吧？

天天：圣诞节快到了，很多商场正在打折，所以价钱跟网上商店的一样便宜。
dǎ zhé　jiàqián

本：　是吗？我要去商场给妹妹买圣诞节的礼物。她的手表坏了，我准备送她一块新手表。
sòng　kuài　shǒubiǎo

天天：商场有很多漂亮的手表，一定有你妹妹喜欢的。

本：　下课后我们去看看吧。

天天：好，我也看看衣服和鞋，要是有合适的我也买。

有时候广告很有用

有的人不喜欢广告，因为广告信息常常不是真的。可是我觉得有时候广告很有用，能给我们一些新商品的信息。上星期我在网上买了一辆自行车。这是我的朋友大卫看到广告以后，打电话告诉我的。

现在越来越多的人喜欢在网上买东西。网上商店里什么东西都有，便宜的东西也有，贵的东西也有。我们家很多东西都是在网上买的。去年夏天，伦敦的天气很热，我妈妈在网上买了冰箱 bīngxiāng 和空调，后来还买了一个大电视。这个月，爸爸的生日快到了，妈妈打算在网上买一个数码照相机送给爸爸。爸爸喜欢旅行的时候拍照。我们家有很多他拍的照片，每一张照片都跟杂志上的一样好看。妈妈一直在看照相机的广告，就想给爸爸找一个最满意的。

Exercises

Read 1 Put a cross in the correct box according to Part I of the text.

1) What does Ben want to buy?

A	B	C
A bicycle	A laptop	A watch

2) Why does Tiantian think that sometimes ads are very helpful?

A	B	C
Help people to buy cheap airline tickets	Help people to buy more stuff	Help people to learn about new products and sales

3) Why does Ben ask Tiantian to find an online shop with lower price?

A	B	C
Tiantian runs an online store	Ben is often online	Tiantian often shops online

4) Where do they plan to go shopping after class?

A	B	C
Online store	Store in downtown	Supermarket

5) What does Ben plan to buy for his sister?

A	B	C
A watch	A bicycle	A digital camera

Listen 2 Listen to David and answer the following questions in English.

1) Where will David and his family go next month?

....

2) What was his mother looking for online?

....

3) What would be their tour route in China?

....

4) How did his mother find the lowest price hotel?

....

5) What did his mother find for him and his brother?

....

6) What did they order online and how did they bring it back to the UK?

....

Read 3 Put a cross to the five correct answers according to Part II of the text

A He thought ads disturbed his life.	
B He bought a bicycle online last week.	
C David found the information and sent me an email.	
D People could only buy some cheap stuff online.	
E His mother bought some electrical appliances online.	
F His mother planned to buy a digital camera for his father.	
G His father likes to take photographs during the journey.	

Talk 4 Read the following paragraph and answer the questions below in Chinese.

　　妹妹想给她的猫买一些鱼，她的朋友想给小狗买一件冬天穿的衣服，她们让我帮助在网上找找卖这些商品的商店。我看过一个网上宠物（chǒngwù，pet）商店的广告，就告诉了她。我想她一定能买到她们想要的东西。妹妹的小猫很可爱，跟电影里的猫一样漂亮。妹妹说，如果商店有宠物电影的DVD，她也想买，她说她会和小猫一起看。

1) What did 'my' sister ask 'me' to do?

....

2) Where did 'my' sister want to buy those things?

....

3) What did 'my' sister's friend want to buy?

....

4) How is 'my' sister's cat?

....

5) What did 'my' sister also want to buy from the online store?

....

Talk 5 You are asked to help a senior relative make a hotel reservation. Please show how to figure it out.

1）How to find an online travel website.　　2）How to compare the prices of different hotels.

3）How to make the reservation.　　4）How to save the information of the hotel.

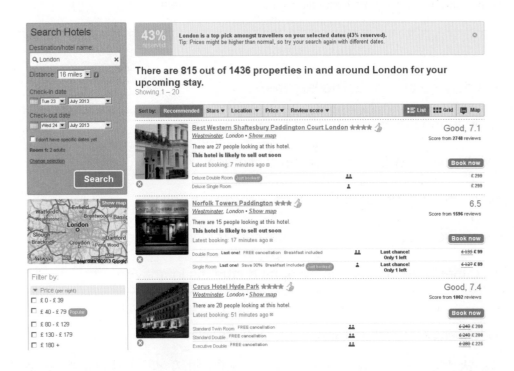

Write 6

Essay Plan Form

Essay title:

Prepare a copy of travel tips upon your return from abroad.

1) How to look for cheaper flights through advertisements

2) How to book cheaper hotels online

| 3) How to look for a few local friends |
| 4) How to find good restaurants |
| 5) How to look for a local specialty store |

| Your conclusion |

Read 7 Reorganize the following sentences and create a short paragraph.

1）妈妈打算在网上买一个数码照相机送给爸爸，因为爸爸喜欢拍照。

2）我们家有很多他拍的照片。

3）现在越来越多的人们喜欢在网上买东西。

4）妈妈差不多天天上网看照相机，就想给爸爸找一个最满意的。

5）爸爸的生日快到了。

6）我们家很多东西都是在网上买的。

中国的少数民族

　　中国自古以来就是一个统一的多民族国家。新中国成立后，通过识别并经中央政府确认的民族共有56个。由于汉族以外的55个民族相对汉族人口较少，习惯上被称为"少数民族"。少数民族占全国总人口的6.6%，分布在中国总面积50~60%的土地上。人口数量居前的少数民族有壮族、满族、回族、苗、维吾尔族、蒙族、藏族等。

Ethnic Groups in China

China has been a unified multi-ethnic country since ancient times. The PRC government has identified 56 ethnic groups; besides the majority Han Chinese, 55 other groups are classified as ethnic minority groups, accounting for 6.6 % of the country's total population and are distributed over 50% to 60% of the area of China. The largest ethnic groups after the Han are the Zhuang, the Manchu, the Hui, the Miao, the Uyghur, the Mongol, and the Tibetan.

第六单元小结　Unit Six Summary

1	名词＋是＋形容词(某处)＋特产。 Noun + 是 + somewhere + famous souvenir.	风筝是这里的特产。 Kites are pieces of local heritage here. 熊猫是中国的特产。 The panda is emblematic of China.
2	某人＋用＋信用卡（＋付钱）（＋动词词组）。 Sb. + 用 + 信用卡 (+ to pay) (+ verb phrase).	我可以用信用卡付钱吗? Can I pay with a credit card? 我用信用卡买书。 I used a credit card to buy books.
3	主语＋形容词＋不＋形容词＋? Subject + adjective + auxiliary word 不 + adjective + ?	地铁票贵不贵? Is the subway ticket expensive? 手表贵不贵? Is the watch expensive? 这本书便宜不便宜? Is this book expensive?
4	火车＋时间词＋开。 Train + time noun + 开.	火车几点开? When will the train leave? 火车半个小时以后开。 The train will leave in half an hour.
5	A也有，B也有。 A 也有 , B 也有.	白色的也有，蓝色的也有。 We have this both in white and in blue. 中国朋友也有，外国朋友也有。 We have Chinese friends and foreign friends.
6	A跟B一样（＋形容词）。 Both A and B (+ adjective).	他的自行车跟我的一样。 His bike is the same as mine. 他拍的照片跟杂志上的一样好看。 The pictures he took are as good as the ones in the magazine.

第六单元小结　Unit Six Summary

7	某人₁／物₁＋帮（助）＋某人₂／物₂＋动词词组。 Sb.₁/sth.₁ + 帮（助）+ sb.₂/sth₂ + verb phrase.	我帮你叫服务员吧。 Let me help to get the waiter. 广告帮助我们了解最新的商品。 Ads help us to know about the latest products.
8	某人＋换＋交通工具＋（动词词组）。 Sb. + 换 + means of transport (+ verb phrase).	我换地铁回家。 I transfer to subways to get home. 下了飞机，我换公共汽车去学校。 I transferred to a bus to get to school after getting off the plane.

第十九课 Lesson 19

Homepage of the School
学校主页

www.xiaoyuan.com.cn

Learning Objectives

交际话题 Topic of conversation:

新闻与网络 News and the
Xīnwén yǔ wǎngluò Internet

基本句型 Sentence patterns:

我们给校长回信。

我要下载这本书。

学校主页上还展览学生们
的国画。

校园每日新闻

教育管理
德育教育
学校介绍
校园动态
首页

校长的信 | 学校活动 | 学生作业 | 每天新闻 | 老师小课堂 | 电视电影节目

New Words

1 主页 zhǔyè **n.** homepage
2 内容 nèiróng **n.** content
3 消息 xiāoxi **n.** news
4 设计 shèjì **v./n.** to design; design
5 回（信）huí (xìn) **v.** to reply (letter, mail, phone call, etc.)
6 在线 zàixiàn online

7 电子书 diànzǐshū **n.** e-book
8 下载 xiàzài **v./n.** to download; download
9 最近 zuìjìn **adv.** recently, lately
10 方法 fāngfǎ **n.** method, way
11 视频 shìpín **n.** video
12 国画 guóhuà **n.** traditional Chinese painting
13 展览 zhǎnlǎn **v.** to exhibit

Text

Part I

本： 大海，快来看，学校主页上
zhǔyè
有新内容了。
nèiróng

大海：是吗？我看看。

本： 看看有什么最新消息，有我
xiāoxi
们感兴趣的活动吗？

大海：先看校长给学生们写的信吧！
他说这次设计网页的时候，
shèjì
还请中学生参加了。他希望
我们喜欢这个新主页。

本： 我们给校长回信，告诉他我
huí xìn
们很喜欢这个新主页。

大海：对。网页上还有老师给我们
的作业，真方便。

本： 我找找今天数学课的作业。

大海：找到了，今天数学课的作业
不多。我们还可以看看别的
内容。

本： 在线图书馆里有许多电子书，
zàixiàn　　　　　　　　diànzǐshū
都很有意思。

大海：我看到了一本英文故事书，
是老师让我们看的。我要
下载这本书。
xiàzài

本： 我也找一本数学的书，可能对
我的数学作业有帮助。

大海：你看，还有一些新电影，有外
语的，也有中文的。

本： 有历史的，也有科学的。放假
的时候我一定要看这些电影。

大海：我可以告诉我的其他朋友，
让他们也上网看看。

学校的主页有很多新内容

最近（zuìjìn）我们学校的网页上有很多新内容。我和同学们觉得网页内容越来越有意思，所以常常上网看看。

放学以后我们谁都不回家，大家一起在学校的电脑教室里上网。要是你忘了作业的内容，你可以在网页上找到，还有老师告诉我们的一些学习好方法（fāngfǎ），非常方便。网页上还有老师的上课视频（shìpín），要是我们上课的时候听不懂，下课后可以上网学习。

我要发邮件告诉我的朋友们，让他们上我们学校的网页看看。他们都学习汉语，网上有一些很有意思的电影，对他们学习汉语有帮助。我找到一个电影，叫《汉字的故事》，它告诉我们汉字的历史和学习汉字的方法。我的朋友Thomas觉得汉字很难，他一定喜欢这个电影。学校的主页上还展览学生们的国画（guóhuà），我画的作品也在上面。我想，Thomas对这些一定有兴趣。

Exercises

 Read 1 Put a cross in the correct box according to Part I of the text.

1) What are they doing on the Internet?

A	B	C
Playing games	Visiting the homepage of the school	Doing their homework

2) What book does Dahai want to read?

A	B	C
A mathematics book	An English story	A history book

3) What does Dahai want to do?

A	B	C
Visit some other homepages	Tell his friends to visit the homepage	Watch films

Listen 2 You are listening to an introduction of a website. Answer the following questions in English.

1) How does he know of the website? What is the website about?

....

2) How can the website help you if you want to learn a Chinese character?

....

3) What did they do? What's the result?

....

4) Can you talk with the teacher on the website?

....

5) What can you do if you want to find a good way to learn Chinese?

....

Read 3 Put a cross to the five correct answers according to Part II of the text.

A All of the students are interested in the school homepage.

B The students go home right after class to visit the website.

C You can check your homework on the homepage.

D You can review on the homepage because there are some courses.

E You can send emails on the homepage.

F Thomas feels that it's quite difficult to learn Chinese characters.

G I am good at Chinese painting.

H If it's possible I'd like to visit other schools' homepages as well.

Talk 4 Read the following paragraph and answer the questions below in Chinese.

很多人都喜欢上网买东西。他们先上网找到他们想要的东西，了解商品的颜色、大小、多少钱。他们可以在看到商品以后再付钱。上网买东西很方便，也比在商店买便宜。可是我更喜欢去商店。有时候我不买东西，只喜欢在商店里看看这个，看看那个。在商店里你可以试试你喜欢的商品，上网就不能。我姐姐很喜欢上网买东西，因为太方便，太便宜，所以她买了很多，可是有很多东西她买了以后不用。我想这是一个很大的问题。

1) What do people do before they decide to buy something on the Internet?

....

2) How can people get what they ordered on the Internet?

....

3) Do people have to pay before they receive what they want to buy?

....

4) Why do people like shopping on the Internet?

....

5) Do 'I' like to go shopping on the Internet or in the store? Why?

....

6) What is the problem that 'I' think about his/her sister?

....

Talk 5

You are going to tell your family members how to buy things on the Internet. You will talk about:

1) Your favourite shopping website.　　2) How to find the favourite products.

3) How to order and pay.　　4) What to do if one doesn't like the products.

Write 6

Essay Plan Form
Essay title: You are going to invite your Chinese friend to visit your school website. Write an email to tell what he/she can find on the homepage.
1) Your favourite section of the website
2) How to watch a film clip
3) How to write an email to teacher
4) Where to find homework
5) Where to find school activities
Your conclusion

Read
7 Reorganize the following sentences and create a short paragraph.

1）你可以在网页上找到作业的内容，还有老师告诉我们的一些学习好方法，非常方便。

2）我和同学们觉得学校的网页内容越来越有意思。

3）我要发邮件告诉我的朋友们，让他们上我们学校的网页看看。

4）我的朋友Thomas觉得汉字很难，他一定喜欢这个电影。

5）放学后我们谁都不回家，大家一起在学校的电脑教室里上网。

6）我找到一个电影，叫《汉字的故事》，它告诉我们汉字的历史和学习汉字的方法。

第二十课 **Lesson** **20**

My Blog
我的博客

Learning Objectives

交际话题 Topic of conversation:

新闻与网络 News and the
Xīnwén yǔ wǎngluò Internet

基本句型 Sentence patterns:

我的网友越来越多。

我现在有自己的博客了。

他每天晚上都看电子邮件。

网络又快又方便。

New Words

1 博客 bókè **n.** blog, weblog
2 速度 sùdù **n.** speed
3 慢 màn **adj.** slow
4 微博 wēibó **n.** microblog
5 晚安 wǎn'ān Good night.
6 会考 huìkǎo General Certificate
7 为了 wèile **prep.** for; in order to
8 更新 gēngxīn **v.** to update, to renew
9 向 xiàng **prep.** toward, to
10 万 wàn **num.** ten thousand
11 又……又…… yòu...yòu... as well as

Text

Part I

丽丽：大卫，晚上好！你在中国
好吗？我们已经放假了，
你呢？

大卫：我很好。两天以前我们才
放假。

丽丽：你在网上做什么？

大卫：我在跟网友聊天儿。

丽丽：你有很多网友吧？

大卫：我的网友越来越多。

丽丽：他们都是中国人吗？

大卫：有很多是外国人。

丽丽：你们用中文聊天吗？

大卫：我们有时用中文，有时用
英文，有时还用一点法文。

丽丽：我也常常跟网友聊天儿。

大卫：我现在有自己的博客了，
bókè
在上面写了很多有趣的
事情。

丽丽：一定很有意思，快给我你
的博客网址，我要看看。

大卫：好的。请等一下，现在网
络的速度有点慢。
sùdù   màn

丽丽：现在好了，收到了。你的
博客里有大海的照片，他
也有博客吗？

大卫：他有微博，我不知道他的
wēibó
微博网址，你给他发电子
邮件问问吧。

丽丽：他常常上网吗？

大卫：他每天晚上都看电子邮件。

丽丽：你那边很晚了吧？

大卫：已经十一点了，我应该睡
觉了。

丽丽：好的，晚安！
wǎn'ān

大卫：再见！

我们的博客生活

中学会考(huìkǎo)以后，我们学校就放假了。为了(wèile)让我的假期更有意思，我开了自己的博客，每天我都更新(gēngxīn)博客内容。听了好听的音乐，看了好看的电影，去了漂亮的地方，我都写博客。我的博客里也有很多照片，有的是朋友们的，有的是我自己的。我的同学们说，他们一看我的博客，就知道我最近在干什么。

我的同学们都有了自己的博客，小雨看到有意思的书，就写博客向(xiàng)朋友们介绍。大海还开了微博，他特别喜欢发微博，有时他妈妈做了好吃的东西，他也用照片发到微博里。他说，已经有一万(wàn)多人访问过他的微博。假期以后，同学们要去不同的学校读书，不能常常见面了。我想开一个我们班的网页，让我们联系更方便。我同学的哥哥是网络工程师，他可以帮助我们做我们的网页。现在网络又(yòu)快又(yòu)方便，虽然我们不在一个学校了，可是我们能常常联系。

Exercises

Read 1 Put a cross in the correct box according to Part I of the text.

1) Where are David's friends from?

A	B	C
China	Foreign countries	China and foreign countries

2) What is Lily's blog about?

A	B	C
Classes	Holiday life	School activities

3) Why does Lily want to email Dahai?

A	B	C
Just to talk	Asking him his blog address	Asking him to send her his photos

Listen 2 You are listening to an introduction of someone's blog. Answer the following questions in English.

1) Does everyone in the class have a blog?

....

2) What does he think about the other classmates' blogs?

....

3) What is his blog special for?

....

4) What does Dahai do in his blog?

....

5) What do you know about Mary?

....

Read
3 Put a cross to the five correct answers according to Part II of the text.

A He has just created his blog in this holiday.

B He often updates his blog.

C His classmates visit his blog very often.

D Xiaoyu introduced the book she's written.

E Dahai's mother is good at cooking.

F He can see his classmates after holiday.

G His brother can help them to make a new homepage for their class.

H Some classmates will be apart next semester.

Talk
4 Read the following paragraph and answer the questions below in Chinese.

　　我在网上认识了一个朋友，她也是中学生。我们常常在微博上说我们的学校生活。她说她的几个同学不知道微博可以做什么，他们说有名的人要有微博，可是他们只是中学生，自己的生活没有什么可以告诉别人的。我说他们可以看他们感兴趣的新闻，我的朋友说他们只看电视。他们不想知道别人想什么和做什么，也不喜欢让他们知道自己想什么和做什么。我想，不跟别的人联系和交流的人，应该是不快乐的吧？我不能过那样的生活，我会觉得非常无聊。

1) What do some people think about micro-blogging?

....

2) What do some friends do when they want to watch the news?

....

3) Why don't some friends want microblog?

....

4) What do 'I' think about those who don't want to communicate with others?

....

5) Will 'I' have the same life as those friends? Why?

....

Talk 5

You are going to introduce a famous person's blog. You will talk about:

1) The name of the blog.

2) The main content.

3) Your favourite part.

4) Some part you recommend or you hope to improve.

Write 6

Essay Plan Form

Essay title:

Write a short paragraph to talk about your holiday in the blog.

1) Time of the holiday
2) Your plan or your experience
3) Ask some information about your friend's holiday
4) Ask your friend to talk with you or send you some pictures

Your conclusion

Read 7 Reorganize the following sentences and create a short paragraph.

1）假期以后，同学们要去不同的学校读书，不能常常见面了。

2）中学会考以后，我们学校就放假了。

3）我想开一个我们班的网页，让我们联系更方便。

4）为了让我的假期更有意思，我开了自己的博客，每天我都更新博客内容。

5）现在网络又快又方便，虽然我们不在一个学校了，可是我们能常常联系。

6）我的同学们说，他们一看我的博客，就知道我最近在干什么。

第二十一课 Lesson **21**

The Chinese Day
"中国日"活动

Learning Objectives

交际话题 Topic of conversation:

新闻与网络 News and the
Xīnwén yǔ wǎngluò
Internet

基本句型 Sentence patterns:

我还要多练习练习。

祝你们成功!

没想到那天电视台的记者也
来我们学校采访了。

我进学校大门的时候,看见
记者正在采访我的同学。

New Words

1. 练习 liànxí **v.** to exercise
2. 成功 chénggōng **v.** to succeed
3. 太极拳 tàijíquán **n.** Tai Chi, shadow boxing
4. 书法 shūfǎ **n.** calligraphy
5. 画 huà **v.** to draw, to paint
6. 服务 fúwù **n.** service
7. 起(名字)qǐ(míngzi) **v.** to name
8. 采访 cǎifǎng **v.** to interview
9. 棒 bàng **adj.** excellent, good
10. 电视台 diànshìtái **n.** TV station
11. 没想到 méi xiǎngdào not expect

Text

Part I

（小雨和天天在校园里）

小雨：这个周末学校有一个活动，叫"中国日"，你参加吗？

天天：我参加。我的同学Peter打算唱中文歌，他想让我跟他一起唱。

小雨：你们准备得怎么样？

天天：Peter很努力，唱得越来越好，可是我还要多练习练习。
　　　　　liànxí

小雨：Peter的中文很好，你们一定会成功。
　　　　　chénggōng

天天：他说普通话说得很好，唱歌也唱得很好。

小雨：你们班还有别的节目吗？

天天：有很多。有人要打太极拳，
　　　　　　　　tàijíquán
　　　有人要表演书法，听说还有
　　　　　　　　shūfǎ
　　　人要唱京剧。

小雨：那一定很有意思。

天天：我听说还有一个国画展览，好多同学们都画了。

小雨：是的，我也画了。
　　　　　　　huà

天天：是吗？我一定去看你的画。你知道那天学校有介绍中国地理、中国茶、中国风筝的电影吗？

小雨：当然知道。我也让我的爸爸妈妈来看看。

天天：那天，还有一个很特别的服务，中国的老师们还会给
　　　　fúwù
　　　刚学汉语的同学起中文名字。
　　　　　　　　　　　　qǐ

小雨：太好了，我的好朋友还没有中文名字，她知道了一定会来！

天天：明天电视台也会来采访。我要
　　　　　　　　　　　　cǎifǎng
　　　去找Peter练习唱歌了！

小雨：祝你们成功！

我们的"中国日"活动

上个周末，我参加了学校的"中国日"活动，有很多同学都参加了。他们唱中国歌、表演京剧、写书法、画国画、打太极拳，表演得都非常好。我的朋友天天和英国同学Peter用中文唱歌，他们唱得**棒**极
bàng
了。Peter的中文非常好，他说普通话跟中国人一样好。

活动中，我们还看了介绍中国的电影。没想到那天电视台的记者也
méi xiǎngdào　　　　diànshìtái
来我们学校采访了。我进学校大门的时候，看见记者正在采访我的同学。他是法国人，很喜欢唱京剧。他已经学了五年，现在可以当我的京剧老师了。我妈妈的英国朋友Laura Shepherd也跟我一起去学校了。她对中国很感兴趣。我的汉语老师给她起了一个中文名字，她高兴极了。她说以后可以告诉她的中国朋友们，她叫谢乐华，你们觉得这个中文名字怎么样？

Exercises

 Read 1 Put a cross in the correct box according to Part I of the text.

1) What is the activity during the weekend?

A	B	C
Foreign students perform in Chinese	Chinese students perform for others	All students speak Chinese the whole day

2) Who drew the paintings in the exhibition?

A	B	C
Students from every class	Students from Tiantian's class	Students from China

3) Who wants a Chinese name?

A	B	C
Xiaoyu's mother	Xiaoyu's English friend	Xiaoyu's mother's English friend

Listen 2 You are listening to an English boy talking about his Chinese learning. Answer the following questions in English.

1) How long has he learnt Chinese?

....

2) What was his biggest problem at the beginning?

....

3) How did he improve his learning?

....

4) How about his learning now?

....

5) What will he do next month? Why?

....

Read 3 Put a cross to the five correct answers according to Part II of the text.

A All the students attended the competition last weekend.

B Tiantian sing songs in Chinese with his English friend.

C Peter can speak Chinese as good as Chinese people.

D We watched a film introducing China.

E The journalist interviewed the teacher who taught me Peking Opera.

F My French classmate has learnt Peking Opera for five years.

G My mother went to school with me.

H Mum's English friend was happy to have a Chinese name.

Talk 4 Read the following paragraph and answer the questions below in Chinese.

这个学期我们有一个"中国文化周"活动，在一个星期的时间里，每天上午有人来给我们介绍中国的历史、汉语学习、中国最美的地方、好吃的东西、有名的节日；下午老师教我们做风筝、写书法、画国画。老师教我们是免费的，我们做的风筝、写的书法、画的国画也可以带（dài, to take）回家给爸爸妈妈和朋友们看。我参加了做风筝的活动，我很努力地学，最后做了一个非常漂亮的鱼风筝，老师和我都非常满意。别的很多同学也给我看了他们画的国画、写的书法，他们做得都很棒！

1) What can you know about China in the morning?

2) What can you do in the afternoon?

3) What did 'I' do? What was the result?

4) What did other classmates do? What did 'I' think about them?

5) Can you tell what the activity is now? How long did it last?

Talk 5

You are going to plan a party for some Chinese students to introduce English culture. You will talk about:

1）The most famous thing in English culture.

2）Things you like about English culture.

3）Some activities that the Chinese students can join.

4）Something that the Chinese students can take or keep.

5）Time and cost to travel in Britain.

Essay Plan Form

Essay title:

You are going to interview someone about a festival celebration in your school. Write a list of your questions.

1) The theme of this celebration

2) People who will participate

3) What people can do

4) The activities of that day

5) How to give organizer the feedback

Your conclusion

Read 7 Reorganize the following sentences and create a short paragraph.

1）我的朋友天天和英国同学Peter用中文唱歌，他们唱得很棒。

2）她叫谢乐华，你们觉得这个中文名字怎么样？

3）我妈妈的朋友*Laura Shepherd*也跟我一起去学校了。

4）活动中，我们还看了介绍中国的电影。

5）上个周末，我参加了学校的"中国日"活动，有很多同学都参加了。

6）我的汉语老师给她起了一个中文名字，她高兴极了。

7）那天电视台的记者也来我们学校采访了。我进学校大门的时候，看见记者正在采访我们班的同学。

中国的四大名著

中国的四大名著是指四部古典小说《三国演义》、《水浒传》、《西游记》、《红楼梦》的统称。《三国演义》反映了三国时代的政治军事斗争，概括了这一时代的历史巨变。《水浒传》以古代绿林好汉为题材，刻画了众多人物。《西游记》写了孙悟空随唐僧西天取经，沿途除妖降魔、战胜困难的故事。《红楼梦》描写了几个大家族的盛衰，讲述了主人公贾宝玉、林黛玉的爱情悲剧，反映出当时的社会现状，是中国古典小说的巅峰之作。

Four Great Classical Novels of Chinese Literature

The four great classical novels of Chinese literature are *Romance of the Three Kingdoms*, *Outlaws of the Marsh*, *Journey to the West*, and *Dream of the Red Chamber*. *Romance of the Three Kingdoms* is a historical novel about the turbulent years and historical changes near the end of the Han Dynasty and the Three Kingdoms era of Chinese history. *Outlaws of the Marsh* tells a folk story of a group of 108 outlaws, and also introduces many other literary characters to readers. *Journey to the West* tells the story of how Xuan Zang, a Buddhist monk of the Tang Dynasty, assisted by his three disciples, endured countless difficulties imposed by various monsters and demons, and finally travelled to India in search of the Buddhist Sutras. *Dream of the Red Chamber* is generally acknowledged as the pinnacle of Chinese classic fiction. With the tragic love story of Jia Baoyu and Lin Daiyu as the main theme, the novel describes the decline of four feudal noble families and reflects upon the social conditions of the Qing Dynasty.

第七单元小结　Unit Seven　Summary

1　某人＋越来越＋动词。 Sb. + 越来越 + verb.	他越来越喜欢在线学习。 He likes studying online more and more. 我越来越想了解他们的文化。 I want to learn about their culture more and more.
2　又＋形容词₁／副词₁＋又＋形容词₂／副词₂…… 又 + adjective₁/adverb₁ + 又 + adjective₂/adverb₂….	网络又快又方便。 The Internet is fast as well as convenient. 他说得又快又清楚。 He speaks fast and clear.
3　为了……，某人…… In order to do sth., sb.….	为了参加中学会考，大家都在努力学习。 Students are studying hard for the GCSE. 为了让身体更健康，他每天都运动。 He exercises everyday in order to have a fit body.
4　某人＋动词₁＋名词＋动词₂＋得＋形容词。 Sb. + verb₁ + noun + verb₂ + auxiliary word 得 + adjective.	他说普通话说得很好。 He speaks good Mandarin. 你画国画画得真棒。 You are really good at traditional Chinese painting.
5　某人₁＋动词词组₁＋的时候，某人₂＋正在＋动词词组₂。 Sb.₁ + verb phrase₁ + 的时候，sb.₂ + 正在 + verb phrase₂.	我去学校的时候，他正在采访校长。 He was interviewing the head teacher when I got to school. 你上网的时候，我正在更新我的主页。 I was updating my homepage when you were surfing online.

第二十二课 Lesson

22

Experience of a Part-time Job
兼职经历

Learning Objectives

交际话题 Topic of conversation:
工作与未来 Job and the
Gōngzuò yǔ wèilái Future

基本句型 Sentence patterns:
他从小特别喜欢看书。
我还能赚一些零用钱。
他帮助人们借书和还书。

New Words

1. 沙漠 shāmò **n.** desert
2. 好像 hǎoxiàng **adv.** seem; as if
3. 从小 cóngxiǎo **adv.** from an early age
4. 想起来 xiǎng qǐlái **v.** to remember, to recollect
5. 借 jiè **v.** to borrow
6. 还 huán **v.** to return

7. 台 tái **m.w.** (a measure word to describe TV, etc.)
8. 零用钱 língyòngqián **n.** pocket money
9. 外面 wàimiàn **n.** outside, outdoor
10. 高中 gāozhōng **n.** high school
11. 比较 bǐjiào **adv.** comparatively

Text

Part I

（大海和大卫在聊天儿）

大海：你有没有看昨天晚上的电视？

大卫：我看了新闻节目。

大海：你看到一个中学生记者跟电视台一起去沙漠的采访新闻了吗？
shāmò

大卫：看到了，他们棒极了。

大海：那个记者是我的小学同学。

大卫：真的吗？他太棒了。他很喜欢记者这个工作吧？

大海：对，上小学时他就在电视节目里做过小记者。

大卫：他去过很多地方吧？他好像什么都知道。
hǎoxiàng

大海：他从小特别喜欢看书，看过很多书。
cóngxiǎo

大卫：我想起来了。我看过一个他的节目，介绍他喜欢读的书。那个节目做得非常好。
xiǎng qǐlái

大海：他暑假时也在图书馆工作，帮助人们借书和还书。
jiè huán

大卫：我想他在图书馆一定读了很多书。

大海：我们都觉得将来他会是一个非常成功的记者。

大卫：你们一定常常在一起聊天儿吧？

大海：我很难见到他，他太忙了。可是我们可以常常看到他从很多地方发的博客，写得好极了。

大卫：请给我他的博客地址吧，我也想看看。

我和哥哥都做兼职

这个暑假，我在我家旁边的图书馆做兼职，帮助社区里的孩子们借书、还书。这是一个很好的工作，我可以帮助别人，也可以看很多我喜欢的书，还能赚一些零用钱。以前我不知道，夏天会有很多人来图书馆，有的来借书，有的来看书、看杂志。我想因为天气太热了，人们不喜欢在外面活动，就来图书馆看书了。

我哥哥高中毕业以后，去餐厅当了服务员。这个工作赚钱比较多，他希望能用自己的钱买一台电脑。现在他在一家意大利餐厅工作，还学会了做意大利菜。昨天晚上他给我们全家做了意大利面条，我们都吃得很高兴。妈妈说哥哥做的面条比她做的好吃。她觉得我们开始兼职以后学会做很多事情。

Exercises

 Read 1 Put a cross in the correct box according to Part I of the text.

1) How does Dahai know the journalist?

A	B	C
They went to the same middle school.	They went to the same primary school.	He is quite famous.

2) Why don't they meet very often?

A	B	C
They both have part-time jobs and they're busy.	They prefer to communicate through blogging.	The journalist is quite busy.

3) What does David want to do?

A	B	C
To meet the journalist	To visit his blog	To talk with the journalist

Listen 2 You are listening to a girl talking about her experience of a part-time job. Answer the following questions in English.

1) When does she do her part time job usually?

....

2) Where and what did she teach?

....

3) Why does she think it's not easy to do the job?

....

4) How did she try to improve her work? What's the result?

....

5) What does she think of her work?

....

Read
3

Put a cross to the five correct answers according to Part II of the text.

A He plans to take a part-time job in a library this summer vacation.

B He likes this job because he likes reading and helping people.

C There are few people who come to the library in the summer.

D People come to the library because it's too hot outside in the summer.

E His brother has graduated from high school.

F His brother wants to get more money to go to college.

G His brother is a waiter and learning cooking in an Italian restaurant.

H His mother is satisfied with them because they've learnt so much.

Talk
4

Read the following paragraph and answer the questions below in Chinese.

我的朋友冰冰在学校的电视台的一个节目里说新闻，大家都喜欢看。我和她一起去过电视台，我很喜欢她的工作，也常常跟冰冰聊那里的工作，她也教我一些说新闻的方法。这个星期冰冰感冒了，她请了假。可是谁去说新闻呢？她想介绍我去。虽然我还没有经验，但是我会努力练习。冰冰总是帮助我。我说新闻的那天，我紧张极了。可是大家对我说的新闻很满意，这真是没想到。

1) What does Bingbing do?

....

2) What happened to Bingbing this week?

....

3) What did Bingbing ask 'me' to do?

....

4) What did 'I' worry about?

....

5) What did 'I' do for the work? What's the result?

....

Talk 5 You are going to tell of the experience of a part-time job of yours or your friend's. You will talk about:

1) When and where you or your friend had that part-time job.   2) Something you're good at or not.

3) What impressed you or your friend the most.   4) Your achievement.

Write 6

Essay Plan Form
Essay title:
Write a blog to talk about the experience of your part-time job.
1) Time and location
2) What you've done in the part-time job
3) Your gain and discoveries
4) Your suggestion or advice for other people
Your conclusion

Read
7

Reorganize the following sentences and create a short paragraph.

1）我哥哥高中毕业以后，去餐厅当了服务员。

2）以前我不知道，夏天会有很多人来图书馆，有的来借书，有的来看书、看杂志。

3）这个暑假，我在我家旁边的图书馆做兼职，帮助社区里的孩子们借书、还书。

4）他在一个意大利餐厅工作，还学会了做意大利菜。

5）这是一个很好的工作，我可以帮助别人，也可以看很多我喜欢的书。

6）这个工作赚钱比较多，他希望能用自己的钱买一台电脑。

7）我想因为天气太热了，人们不喜欢在外面活动，就来图书馆看书了。

第二十三课 Lesson **23**

I Want to Teach English
我想教英语

Learning Objectives

交际话题 Topic of conversation:
工作与未来 Job and the
Gōngzuò yǔ wèilái Future

基本句型 Sentence patterns:
我非常希望自己能得到这个
工作。
我们需要面试一下。
面试结束后，校长让我们
等他的邮件。

New Words

1 姓名 xìngmíng **n.** full name

2 国籍 guójí **n.** nationality

3 需要 xūyào **v.** to need

4 游戏 yóuxì **n.** game

5 只 zhǐ **adv.** only, just

6 得到 dédào **v.** to get, to obtain

7 结束 jiéshù **v.** to finish; to be over

Text

Part I

（在小学校长的办公室）

大卫：你好！我是来申请兼职工作的。

校长：你想申请什么工作？

大卫：我想教孩子们英语。

校长：你有没有做过兼职工作？

大卫：去年署假，我教过一个五岁孩子学英语，他很喜欢我的课。

校长：请告诉我，你的姓名和
xìngmíng
国籍。
guójí

大卫：我叫大卫，我是英国人，一年前我爸爸来中国工作，我们全家跟他一起来了。

校长：你还做过别的兼职吗？

大卫：没有了，去年夏天的兼职是我的第一个工作。

校长：你能告诉我，你为什么要申请这个工作？

大卫：我很喜欢做教师。我妈妈是教师，我觉得她和学生在一起的时候总是很快乐。

校长：你知道这个工作的内容吗？

大卫：我看了你们的广告，这个工作需要用英语跟孩子们交流、
xūyào
做游戏。

校长：对。还有几个人也申请了这个工作，有英国人，也有美国人。我们需要面试一下。

大卫：什么时候？

校长：明天下午两点。

Part II

兼职面试

　　昨天下午我参加了兼职工作的面试，有五个人申请这个工作，两个英国人，两个美国人，还有一个日本人。这个学校需要一个英语教师和一个日语教师，上课时间是星期一到星期四的下午，老师要用外语跟孩子们一起唱歌、做游戏。我们四个说英语的人只有一个工作的机会，那 zhǐ 个日本人比较容易得到这个工作。我非常希望自己能得到这个工作，因 dédào 为我对教英语很有兴趣，我可以让那些孩子们的英语一天比一天好。为了准备这次面试，我还设计了几个学英语的小游戏，练习了英文歌。我想让校长知道，我一定会是一个好老师，孩子们会喜欢我的。面试结束 jiéshù 后，校长让我们等他的邮件，我希望得到的是好消息。

Exercises

 Put a cross in the correct box according to Part I of the text.

1) What did David do before?

A	B	C
Taught five boys English	Taught a five-year-old boy English	Taught a boy five English lessons

2) Where are they talking?

A	B	C
In a Chinese school	In an English school	In an American school

3) What does David need to do for the part-time job?

A	B	C
Teach the children English in Chinese	Explain some advertisement in English to the children	Play games with the children in English

Listen 2 You are listening to a boy talking about his experience in applying for a part-time job. Answer the following questions in English.

1) Where can they get the information for applying for a part-time job?

....

2) What is the part-time job about?

....

3) What does he need to do if he wants to get a part-time job?

....

4) What are the questions included in the interview?

....

5) What do his family members think of his applying for a part-time job?

....

Read 3 Put a cross to the five correct answers according to Part II of the text.

A He started his part-time job yesterday afternoon.

B There were four English speakers applying for the part-time job.

C The only Japanese speaker would certainly get the part-time job.

D　They needed to play games with the children in English every afternoon.

E　He likes to help children to improve their English.

F　He prepared some English games and practised some English songs for the interview.

G　He wanted to convince the school headmaster that he fits the job.

H　He received the headmaster's email telling him that he got the part-time job.

Talk 4　Read the following paragraph and answer the questions below in Chinese.

　　我家在中国的上海。去年我妈妈来英国工作，我也跟她一起来了，在这里的一个中学学习。这个学校有很多学生活动。今年我在学校的体育活动办公室做兼职，给学生们介绍中国的太极拳。他们非常高兴有我做这个工作，因为越来越多的学生对太极拳感兴趣，希望能学一点儿。我从五岁开始学习太极拳，在中国的小学和中学就得过学校太极拳比赛的第一名。我也很高兴有这个机会给外国人介绍太极拳。现在学习太极拳的有十几个学生，还有三四个老师，大家每个星期练习一个小时太极拳。他们有的打得非常好，有的打得不太好，可是大家都非常努力，也觉得很快乐。

1) Where am 'I' now?

....

2) What do 'I' do for the part-time job?

....

3) Why was 'I' invited to do this job?

....

4) Who is attending the activity?

....

5) How long do 'I' need to work per week? And how do people feel about 'me'?

....

Talk 5

You are going to go through a job interview. You will talk about:

1）The job you're going to apply for.

2）What you know about the job.

3）Convince the interviewer that you would fit the job, including your experience, your background knowledge, some qualifications, etc.

Write 6

Essay Plan Form

| Essay title: |
| An email to apply for a part-time job. |

| 1) The position you're going to apply |
| 2) Your personal information |
| 3) Your previous working experience |
| 4) You wish to get the job |

| Your conclusion |

Read 7 Reorganize the following sentences and create a short paragraph.

1）我对教英语很有兴趣，我可以让那些孩子们的英语一天比一天好。

2）面试结束后，校长让我们等他的邮件，我希望得到的是好消息。

3）这个学校需要一个英语教师和一个日语教师，上课时间是星期一到星期四的下午，老师要用外语跟孩子们一起唱歌、做游戏。

4）为了准备这次面试，我还设计了几个学英语的小游戏，练习了英文歌。

5）我们四个说英语的人只有一个工作机会，那个日本人比较容易得到这个工作。

6）我想让校长知道，我一定会是一个好老师，孩子们会喜欢我的。

7）我非常希望自己能得到这个工作，因为我对教英语很有兴趣。

第二十四课 Lesson

24

Ideal University
理想的大学

交际话题 Topic of conversation:

工作与未来 Job and the
Gōngzuò yǔ wèilái   Future

基本句型 Sentence patterns:

听说那所大学出了很多名人。

校园里又漂亮又安静。

我现在对历史很有兴趣，以后可能就变了。

New Words

1 南方 nánfāng **n.** south; in the south of china

2 开学 kāi xué school begins

3 所 suǒ **m.w.** (a measure word for school, university)

4 出 chū **v.** to produce

5 学院 xuéyuàn **n.** college

6 安静 ānjìng **adj.** quiet

7 校园 xiàoyuán **n.** campus

8 专业 zhuānyè **n.** major, subject

9 决定 juédìng **v.** to decide

10 可能 kěnéng **adv.** maybe, perhaps

11 变 biàn **v.** to change

12 上传 shàngchuán **v.** to upload

13 谈谈 tántan **v.** to talk

Text

Part I

小雨：京京，你哥哥去哪儿了？我很久没看见他了。

京京：他去南方上大学了。
nánfāng

小雨：他什么时候走的？

京京：8月31号。学校是9月1号开学。
kāi xué

小雨：那所大学很有名吗？
suǒ

京京：是的。听说那所大学出了
chū
很多名人。

小雨：你去过那所大学吗？

京京：我跟我哥哥一起去了，他们的学院又漂亮又安静。
xuéyuàn   ānjìng

小雨：你哥哥一定很满意那里吧？

京京：是的，我也很喜欢那个校园。
xiàoyuán

小雨：你哥哥学习什么专业？
zhuānyè

京京：他学习数学，他的数学学得特别好。

小雨：你呢，你打算将来学什么专业？

京京：我觉得地理很有意思，我想学地理。

小雨：你想上你哥哥那所大学吗？

京京：我希望能上那所大学。你呢，打算学什么专业？

小雨：现在还没决定，等上了高中
juédìng
以后再决定。我现在对历史很有兴趣，以后可能就变了。
kěnéng   biàn

京京的哥哥上大学了

京京的哥哥去南方上大学了。那是一所很有名的大学，有很多很好的专业。她跟哥哥一起去参观了那所大学，校园里又漂亮又安静，她拍了很多校园里的照片，上传 到了网上。如果你有兴趣，可以上她的博客看看。

上传
shàngchuán

今年夏天我参加了中学会考。秋天的时候，我就要上高中了。我会努力学习，三年以后，我也要上大学。我特别喜欢读历史书，所以我想将来学历史专业。可是有人说这个专业不容易找工作，应该学习电脑、网络这些容易找工作的专业。可是我的数学不好，不能学这些专业，我也不太喜欢。哪个专业又有意思又好找工作呢？我要找时间跟老师谈谈 这个问题，我想一定会有我喜欢的专业。

谈谈
tántan

Exercises

Read 1 Put a cross in the correct box according to Part I of the text.

1) Where did Jingjing's brother go for university?

A	B	C
His hometown	One in the south of China	One in the north of China

2) What major did her brother study?

A	B	C
Maths	Science	Geography

3) What is Xiaoyu interested in now?

A	B	C
Maths	Geography	History

Listen 2 You are listening to a Chinese girl talking about her ideal university and major. Answer the following questions in English.

1) When will she graduate from her high school?

....

2) What major does she want to study?

....

3) Where does she want to go if it's possible? Why?

....

4) What is the opinion of her parents? Why?

....

5) What does she think about her decision?

....

Read
3
Put a cross to the five correct answers according to Part II of the text.

A The university that Jingjing's brother went to is very famous.

B Jingjing showed me the picture of the university campus.

C Jingjing and Xiaoyu will be in high school in this summer.

D Her favourite course is history.

E Someone suggested that she should study computer engineering to easily find a job.

F She doesn't like maths at all.

G She thinks it's impossible to find an easy and interesting job.

H She wants to discuss her major with her teacher.

Talk
4
Read the following paragraph and answer the questions below in Chinese.

　　我是一个很安静的女孩，现在上高中二年级，明年我就要中学毕业，可还没决定大学上什么专业。我喜欢语言，可是很多同学都说语言专业没有意思，将来也不容易找到好工作。我也喜欢图书馆专业，可是同学们说图书馆专业太无聊了。他们有的喜欢网络、新闻，有的喜欢表演、旅游，有的喜欢和环境、工程有关系的专业，学那些专业将来容易找工作，又有意思又能赚钱。我问过爸爸妈妈，他们说只希望我快乐。我有一个同学的姐姐在博物馆工作，她有机会跟许多国家的人交流，所以学习了多种语言，也常常需要在图书馆读很多书。我对历史也感兴趣，将来在博物馆工作可能也很好。

1) What do 'my' classmates think about language major?

....

2) What kind of majors do they prefer? Why?

....

3) What's 'my' parents' opinion?

....

4) What am 'I' interested in?

....

5) What might 'my' future job be? Why?

....

Talk 5 You are going to talk about your favourite university. You will talk about:

1) The name and location of this university.

2) What it's famous for.

3) Your favourite major and the reason.

4) Your courses.

Write 6

Essay Plan Form

Essay title:
An email to a friend to suggest two good universities in your city or country.

1) Your personal opinion

2) The reasons you suggest these two universities

3) What the campuses look like

4) What majors of the two universities offer

Your conclusion

Read 7 Reorganize the following sentences and create a short paragraph.

1）我特别喜欢读历史书，所以我想将来学历史专业。

2）今年夏天我们参加了中学会考，秋天的时候，我就要上高中了。

3）哪个专业又有意思又好找工作呢？

4）可是有人说这个专业不容易找工作，应该学习电脑、网络这些容易找工作的专业。

5）我要找时间跟老师谈谈这个问题，我想一定会有我喜欢的专业。

6）三年以后，我也要上大学。

7）可是我的数学不太好，不能学这些专业。

文化常识 Cultural Tip

岁寒三友

　　岁寒三友指松、竹、梅三种植物。因这三种植物在寒冬时节仍可保持顽强的生命力而得名，是中国传统文化中高尚人格的象征，也借以比喻忠贞的友谊。松竹梅合成的岁寒三友图案是中国古代器物、衣物和建筑上常用的装饰题材。同时岁寒三友还是中国画的常见题材，画作常以"三友图"命名。

Three Friends of Winter

The Three Friends of Winter refer to pine, bamboo, and plum. The three plants are noted for their durability in cold weather, and can still thrive when many other plants begin to wither. Together they symbolise perseverance, integrity, and modesty in traditional Chinese culture. The Three Friends of Winter are commonly seen in works of Chinese art, on household objects such as textiles, and in architectural designs. They are also some of the most popular themes in traditional Chinese paintings.

第八单元小结 Unit Eight Job and the Future	
1 某人＋有没有＋动词＋过＋名词。 Sb. + 有没有 + verb + 过 + noun.	你有没有做过记者？ Have you ever been a reporter before? 你们有没有学过书法？ Have you ever learnt calligraphy before?
2 某人₁＋教＋某人₂＋动词词组。 Sb.₁ + 教 + sb.₂ + verb phrase.	老师教我们说中文。 The teacher taught us how to speak Chinese. 他教一个孩子学日语。 He taught a kid Japanese.
3 某人＋只＋动词词组。 Sb. + 只 + verb phrase.	我只吃蔬菜。 I only eat vegetables. 他们只上一个小时汉语课。 They have Chinese class only for an hour.
4 名词₁＋出（了）＋名词₂。 Noun₁ + 出（了）+ noun₂.	这里出水果。 This place is famous for its fruits. 这所大学出了很多名人。 A lot of famous people have graduated from this university.
5 主语＋的确＋…… Subject + 的确 + ...	他的确很有名。 He is indeed a celebrity. 这的确是一个理想的工作。 This is indeed an ideal job.
6 某人＋去过＋某处＋疑问词＋？ 某人＋去过／没去过。 Sb. + 去过 + somewhere + interrogative word + ? Sb. + 去过／没去过.	你去过中国吗？我没去过。 Have you ever been to China? No, I haven't. 你去过那所大学吗？ Have you ever been to that university?

Appendix: Vocabulary Lists

A. Chinese-English Vocabulary List

生字词	拼音	词性	英文	页码
爱	ài	v.	to like, to love	49
安静	ānjìng	adj.	quiet	183
白	bái	adj.	white	97
百	bǎi	num.	hundred	104
百货公司	bǎihuò gōngsī	n.	department store	39
办公室	bàngōngshì	n.	office	39
棒	bàng	adj.	excellent, good	159
比较	bǐjiào	adv.	comparatively	169
比如	bǐrú	v.	such as	87
毕业	bìyè	v./n.	to graduate; graduation	15
变	biàn	v.	to change	183
别的	biéde	pron.	other	8
冰箱	bīngxiāng	n.	refrigerator	135
博客	bókè	n.	bolg, weblog	152
博物馆	bówùguǎn	n.	museum	25
不同	bù tóng	adj.	different	1
才	cái	adv.	then and only then	80
采访	cǎifǎng	v.	to interview	159
参观	cānguān	v.	to visit	56
参加	cānjiā	v.	to join	73
餐厅	cāntīng	n.	restaurant	49
查看	chákàn	v.	to check; to look up	80
成功	chénggōng	v.	to succeed	159
成人	chéngrén	n.	adult	128
宠物	chǒngwù	n.	pet	63
出	chū	v.	to produce	183
出生	chūshēng	v.	to be born	8
穿	chuān	v.	to wear	63
船	chuán	n.	boat, ship	56

生字词	拼音	词性	英文	页码
从小	cóngxiǎo	adv.	from an early age	169
聪明	cōngming	adj.	clever, intelligent	15
错	cuò	adj.	wrong	73
打折	dǎ zhé	v.	to have a discount	135
大家	dàjiā	n.	everyone	87
大约	dàyuē	adv.	about, approximately	56
带	dài	v.	to bring, to take	
但是	dànshì	conj.	but, yet, however	8
当天	dàngtiān		that very day	97
导游	dǎoyóu	n.	tour guide	8
得到	dédào	v.	to get, to obtain	176
的确	díquè	adv.	indeed	183
等等	děngděng	part.	etc.; and so on	56
地铁	dìtiě	n.	subway, underground, tube	39
点菜	diǎn cài	v.	to order dishes	121
电视台	diànshìtái	n.	TV station	159
电子书	diànzǐshū	n.	e-book	145
懂	dǒng	v.	to know, to understand	73
动物园	dòngwùyuán	n.	zoo	56
杜甫	Dù Fǔ		Du Fu, an ancient Chinese poet	104
端午节	Duānwǔ Jié	n.	Dragon Boat Festival	49
短	duǎn	adj.	short	111
队	duì	n.	team	97
对	duì	adj.	right	73
饿	è	adj.	hungry	49
饭	fàn	n.	meal	121
方便	fāngbiàn	adj.	convenient	39
方法	fāngfǎ	n.	method, way	73
房子	fángzi	n.	house, building	25
分别	fēnbié	adv.	seperately	87
粉丝	fěnsī	n.	fan	97
份	fèn	m.w.	(a measure word used for papers)	15
风筝	fēngzheng	n.	kite	121

生字词	拼音	词性	英文	页码
服务	fúwù	n.	service	159
付钱	fù qián	v.	to pay	121
刚才	gāngcái	n.	just now	87
高中	gāozhōng	n.	high school	169
更	gèng	adv.	even more	87
更新	gēngxīn	v.	to update, to renew	152
工厂	gōngchǎng	n.	factory	15
公园	gōngyuán	n.	park	25
古代	gǔdài	n.	ancient times	39
国画	guóhuà	n.	traditional Chinese painting	145
国籍	guójí	n.	nationality	176
海	hǎi	n.	sea	56
好像	hǎoxiàng	adv.	seem; as if	169
合适	héshì	adj.	suitable, appropriate	15
后来	hòulái	adv.	later	73
湖	hú	n.	lake	32
护照	hùzhào	n.	passport	121
花	huā	v.	to spend	73
华人	huárén	n.	Chinese people	97
滑冰	huá bīng	n./v.	skating; to skate	56
画	huà	v.	to draw, to paint	159
话题	huàtí	n.	topic, subject (of a talk or conversation)	1
还	huán	v.	to return	169
环境	huánjìng	n.	environment, circumstances	39
换	huàn	v.	to change, to exchange	128
回（信）	huí (xìn)	v.	to reply (letter, mail, phone call, etc.)	145
回答	huídá	v./n.	to answer; answer	87
回国	huí guó		to return to sb's mother country	128
会	huì	v.	can; to be able to	80
会考	huìkǎo		General Certificate	152
或者	huòzhě	conj.	or	39
机会	jīhuì	n.	chance, opportunity	80
记	jì	v.	to remember	73

生字词	拼音	词性	英文	页码
纪念	jìniàn	v.	to remember	104
继续	jìxù	v.	to go on; to continue	87
寄	jì	v.	to send, to post	32
价钱	jiàqián	n.	price	135
检查	jiǎnchá	n./v.	check; to check	63
件	jiàn	m.w.	(a measure word used for clothing)	111
交流	jiāoliú	v.	to exchange	1
交通	jiāotōng	n.	traffic, transportation	39
教堂	jiàotáng	n.	church, temple, cathedral	32
接	jiē	v.	to pick up	97
结束	jiéshù	v.	to finish; to be over	176
解决	jiějué	v.	to solve	128
借	jiè	v.	to borrow	169
进步	jìnbù	n./v.	improvement; to improve	73
警察局	jǐngchájú	n.	police bureau; police station; police department	39
酒	jiǔ	n.	wine, alcohol	49
酒店	jiǔdiàn	n.	hotel	121
句	jù	n.	sentence	87
决定	juédìng	v.	to decide	183
开学	kāi xué		school begins	183
可爱	kě'ài	adj.	lovely, lovable	15
可能	kěnéng	adv.	maybe, perhaps	183
可以	kěyǐ	aux.	can, may	1
渴	kě	adj.	thirsty	49
空调	kōngtiáo	n.	air-conditioning	121
空气	kōngqì	n.	air	39
裤子	kùzi	n.	trousers	111
块	kuài	m.w.	(a measure word used for watches)	135
快乐	kuàilè	adj.	happy	56
筷子	kuàizi	n.	chopstick	49
来自	láizì	v.	to come from	1
蓝	lán	adj.	blue	97
老人	lǎorén	n.	senior	49

生字词	拼音	词性	英文	页码
离	lí	v.	to be away from; to leave; to part from	32
李白	Lǐ Bái		Li Bai, an ancient Chinese poet	104
联系	liánxì	v.	to get in touch with; to contact	1
练习	liànxí	n./v.	practice; to practise	73
练习	liànxí	v.	to exercise	159
量	liáng	v.	to check	63
了解	liǎojiě	v.	to know	135
林书豪	Lín Shūháo		Jeremy Lin, a famous basketball player	97
零用钱	língyòngqián	n.	pocket money	169
龙舟	lóngzhōu	n.	dragon boat	104
路	lù	n.	road, path, way	1
路人	lùrén	n.	passerby	121
马上	mǎshàng	adv.	right away	73
卖	mài	v.	to sell	135
满意	mǎnyì	adj.	satisfied, pleased	8
慢	màn	adj.	slow	152
忙	máng	adj.	busy	80
毛衣	máoyī	n.	sweater	111
没想到	méi xiǎngdào		not expect	159
免费	miǎnfèi	v.	to be free	32
名	míng	m.w.	(a measure word used for persons)	15
名片	míngpiàn	n.	name card; (business) card	1
名人	míngrén	n.	celebrity	104
明星	míngxīng	n.	star	97
内容	nèiróng	n.	content	145
那么	nàme	pron.	like that; in that way; then	25
南方	nánfāng	n.	south; in the south of China	183
年	nián	n.	year	8
年轻人	niánqīngrén	n.	young people	63
纽约	Niǔyuē	n.	New York City	97
农历	nónglì	n.	the tradional Chinese calendar	104
努力	nǔlì	adv.	hard	8
拍	pāi	v.	to take (a picture, photograph)	15

生字词	拼音	词性	英文	页码
片	piàn	m.w.	(a measure word used for pills)	63
普通话	Pǔtōnghuà	n.	Putonghua; Mandarin Chinese	15
起（名字）	qǐ(míngzi)	v.	to name	159
千	qiān	num.	thousand	104
前台	qiántái	n.	information and reception counter	121
桥	qiáo	n.	bridge	32
屈原	Qū Yuán		Qu Yuan, an ancient Chinese poet	104
全家	quán jiā		the whole family	128
裙子	qúnzi	n.	skirt	111
让	ràng	v.	to let	80
日本	Rìběn	n.	Japan	128
日期	rìqī	n.	date	8
日语	Rìyǔ	n.	Japanese	8
肉	ròu	n.	meat	49
如果	rúguǒ	conj.	if; in case	1
散步	sànbù	v.	to go for a walk or stroll	32
沙漠	shāmò	n.	desert	169
莎士比亚	Shāshìbǐyà		William Shakespeare	104
商场	shāngchǎng	n.	shopping mall	111
商店	shāngdiàn	n.	shop, store	135
上传	shàngchuán	v.	to upload	183
设计	shèjì	v./n.	to design; design	145
社区	shèqū	n.	community	25
身体	shēntǐ	n.	body	49
生活	shēnghuó	n.	life	80
诗人	Shīrén	n.	poet	104
十分	shífēn	adv.	very, fully	39
十字路口	shízì lùkǒu	n.	crossroad	87
世界	shìjiè	n.	world, universe	25
视频	shìpín	n.	video	145
试试	shìshi	v.	to try, to test	8
收到	shōudào	v.	to receive, to accept	32
手表	shǒubiǎo	n.	watch; wrist watch	135

生字词	拼音	词性	英文	页码
瘦	shòu	adj.	thin, slim	49
书店	shūdiàn	n.	bookstore	111
书法	shūfǎ	n.	calligraphy	159
舒服	shūfu	adj.	comfortable	39
暑假	shǔjià	n.	summer holiday	56
数码	shùmǎ	n.	digital	135
睡觉	shuìjiào	v.	to have a sleep	49
送	sòng	v.	to send	135
速度	sùdù	n.	speed	152
虽然	suīrán	conj.	although; even though	8
所	suǒ	m.w.	(a measure word for school, university)	183
T恤	T-xù	n.	T-shirt	111
台	tái	m.w.	(a measure word to describe TV, etc.)	169
太极拳	tàijíquán	n.	Tai Chi, shadow boxing	159
太太	tàitai	n.	wife	49
太阳	tàiyáng	n.	sun	121
谈谈	tántan	v.	to talk	183
汤	tāng	n.	soup	49
特产	tèchǎn	n.	local specialty	121
体温	tǐwēn	n.	temperature	63
天安门广场	Tiān'ānmén Guǎngchǎng	n.	Tian'anmen Square	25
停	tíng	v.	to stop; to stop over	25
停车场	tíngchēchǎng	n.	parking lot	128
外国	wàiguó	n.	foreign country	1
外面	wàimiàn	n.	outside, outdoor	169
晚安	wǎn'ān		Good night.	152
万	wàn	num.	ten thousand	152
网络	wǎngluò	n.	the Internet	80
网页	wǎngyè	n.	web page	1
网友	wǎngyǒu	n.	net friend	80
网址	wǎngzhǐ	n.	website, (Internet) site	1
忘	wàng	v.	to forget	73

生字词	拼音	词性	英文	页码
微博	wēibó	n.	microblog	152
为了	wèile	prep.	for; in order to	152
文化	wénhuà	n.	culture	111
文学	wénxué	n.	literature	104
文章	wénzhāng	n.	writing, article	15
问题	wèntí	n.	question, problem	128
无聊	wúliáo	adj.	boring	80
西山	Xīshān	n.	Western Hills	56
下一个	xià yí gè	n.	next one	87
下载	xiàzài	v./n.	to download; download	145
想起来	xiǎng qǐlái	v.	to remember, to recollect	169
向	xiàng	prep.	toward, to	152
消息	xiāoxi	n.	news	145
小朋友	xiǎopéngyou	n.	child	63
校园	xiàoyuán	n.	campus	183
笑	xiào	v.	to smile, to laugh	15
鞋	xié	n.	shoes	111
信息	xìnxī	n.	information	135
信用卡	xìnyòngkǎ	n.	credit card	121
行李	xíngli	n.	luggage	121
姓名	xìngmíng	n.	full name	176
熊猫	xióngmāo	n.	panda	56
休闲	xiūxián	adj.	leisure	56
需要	xūyào	v.	to need	176
许多	xǔduō	adj.	many; a lot of	25
学院	xuéyuàn	n.	college	183
颜色	yánsè	n.	colour	97
眼睛	yǎnjing	n.	eye	63
姚明	Yáo Míng		Yao Ming, a famous Chinese basketball player	97
药	yào	n.	medicine	63
要是	yàoshi	conj.	if	73
一下	yíxià		one time	63
衣服	yīfu	n.	clothes	111

生字词	拼音	词性	英文	页码
意大利	Yìdàlì	n.	Italy	128
一直	yìzhí	adv.	straight for ward; all through	25
应该	yīnggāi	v.	should; ought to	63
邮局	yóujú	n.	post office	32
邮票	yóupiào	n.	postage stamp	32
游戏	yóuxì	n.	game	176
游泳池	yóuyǒngchí	n.	swimming pool	32
有用	yǒuyòng	adj.	useful	80
又……又……	yòu...yòu ...		as well as	152
雨伞	yǔsǎn	n.	umbrella	111
语言	yǔyán	n.	language	73
遇到	yùdào	v.	to come across	97
越来越	yuèláiyuè		more and more	73
运动服	yùndòngfú	n.	sportswear	97
再见	zàijiàn		Goodbye.	80
在线	zàixiàn		online	145
展览	zhǎnlǎn	v.	to exhibit	145
展览会	zhǎnlǎnhuì	n.	exhibition	87
赵氏孤儿	Zhàoshì Gū'ér		*Orphan of the Zhao Family,* a Chinese Drama	104
照片	zhàopiàn	n.	photograph, picture	15
照相机	zhàoxiàngjī	n.	camera	111
这些	zhèxiē	pron.	these	1
只	zhǐ	adv.	only, just	176
大学	dàxué	n.	university	15
主页	zhǔyè	n.	homepage	145
住	zhù	v.	to live, to stay	25
专家	zhuānjiā	n.	expert	87
专业	zhuānyè	n.	major, subject	183
赚钱	zhuàn qián	v.	to make money; to make a profit	8
粽子	zòngzi	n.	Zongzi (a traditional food eaten in Dragon Boat Festival)	49
最近	zuìjìn	adv.	recently, lately	145
作品	zuòpǐn	n.	works	104

生字词	拼音	词性	英文	页码
座	zuò	m.w.	(a measure word used mostly for large or fixed objects, e.g. mountains, bridges)	32

Appendix: Vocabulary Lists

B.   **English-Chinese Vocabulary List**

英文	生字词	拼音	词性	页码
(a measure word for school, university)	所	suǒ	m.w.	183
(a measure word to describe TV, etc.)	台	tái	m.w.	169
(a measure word used for clothing)	件	jiàn	m.w.	111
(a measure word used for papers)	份	fèn	m.w.	15
(a measure word used for persons)	名	míng	m.w.	15
(a measure word used mostly for large or fixed objects, e.g. mountains, bridges)	座	zuò	m.w.	32
(a measure word used for pills)	片	piàn	m.w.	63
(a measure word used for watches)	块	kuài	m.w.	135
about, approximately	大约	dàyuē	adv.	56
Orphan of the Zhao Family, a Chinese Drama	赵氏孤儿	zhàoshì Gū'ér		104
adult	成人	chéngrén	n.	128
air	空气	kōngqì	n.	39
air-conditioning	空调	kōngtiáo	n.	121
although; even though	虽然	suīrán	conj.	8
ancient times	古代	gǔdài	n.	39
as well as	又……又……	yòu...yòu ...		152
blue	蓝	lán	adj.	97
boat, ship	船	chuán	n.	56
body	身体	shēntǐ	n.	49
bolg, weblog	博客	bókè	n.	152
bookstore	书店	shūdiàn	n.	111
boring	无聊	wúliáo	adj.	80

英文	生字词	拼音	词性	页码
bridge	桥	qiáo	n.	32
busy	忙	máng	adj.	80
but, yet, however	但是	dànshì	conj.	8
calligraphy	书法	shūfǎ	n.	159
camera	照相机	zhàoxiàngjī	n.	111
campus	校园	xiàoyuán	n.	183
can, may	可以	kěyǐ	aux.	1
can; to be able to	会	huì	v.	80
celebrity	名人	míngrén	n.	104
chance, opportunity	机会	jīhuì	n.	80
check; to check	检查	jiǎnchá	n./v.	63
child	小朋友	xiǎopéngyou	n.	63
Chinese people	华人	huárén	n.	97
chopstick	筷子	kuàizi	n.	49
church, temple, cathedral	教堂	jiàotáng	n.	32
clever, intelligent	聪明	cōngming	adj.	15
clothes	衣服	yīfu	n.	63
college	学院	xuéyuàn	n.	183
colour	颜色	yánsè	n.	97
comfortable	舒服	shūfu	adj.	39
community	社区	shèqū	n.	25
comparatively	比较	bǐjiào	adv.	169
content	内容	nèiróng	n.	145
convenient	方便	fāngbiàn	adj.	39
credit card	信用卡	xìnyòngkǎ	n.	121
crossroad	十字路口	shízì lùkǒu	n.	87
culture	文化	wénhuà	n.	111
date	日期	rìqī	n.	8
department store	百货公司	bǎihuò gōngsī	n.	39
desert	沙漠	shāmò	n.	169
different	不同	bù tóng	adj.	1
digital	数码	shùmǎ	n.	135

英文	生字词	拼音	词性	页码
dragon boat	龙舟	lóngzhōu	n.	104
Dragon Boat Festival	端午节	Duānwǔ Jié	n.	49
Du Fu, an ancient Chinese poet	杜甫	Dù Fǔ		104
e-book	电子书	diànzǐshū	n.	145
environment, circumstances	环境	huánjìng	n.	39
etc.; and so on	等等	děngděng	part.	56
even more	更	gèng	adv.	87
everyone	大家	dàjiā	n.	87
excellent, good	棒	bàng	adj.	159
exhibition	展览会	zhǎnlǎnhuì	n.	87
expert	专家	zhuānjiā	n.	87
eye	眼睛	yǎnjing	n.	63
factory	工厂	gōngchǎng	n.	15
fan	粉丝	fěnsī	n.	97
for; in order to	为了	wèile	prep.	152
foreign country	外国	wàiguó	n.	1
from an early age	从小	cóng xiǎo	adv.	169
full name	姓名	xìngmíng	n.	176
game	游戏	yóuxì	n.	176
General Certificate	会考	huìkǎo		152
Goodbye.	再见	zàijiàn		80
Good night.	晚安	wǎn'ān		152
happy	快乐	kuàilè	adj.	56
hard	努力	nǔlì	adv.	8
high school	高中	gāozhōng	n.	169
homepage	主页	zhǔyè	n.	145
hotel	酒店	jiǔdiàn	n.	121
house, building	房子	fángzi	n.	25
hundred	百	bǎi	num.	104
hungry	饿	è	adj.	49
if	要是	yàoshi	conj.	73
if; in case	如果	rúguǒ	conj.	1

英文	生字词	拼音	词性	页码
improvement; to improve	进步	jìnbù	n./v.	73
indeed	的确	díquè	adv.	183
information	信息	xìnxī	n.	135
information and reception counter	前台	qiántái	n.	121
Italy	意大利	Yìdàlì	n.	128
Japan	日本	Rìběn	n.	128
Japanese	日语	Rìyǔ	n.	8
Jeremy Lin, a famous basketball player	林书豪	Lín Shūháo		97
just now	刚才	gāngcái	n.	87
kite	风筝	fēngzheng	n.	121
lake	湖	hú	n.	32
language	语言	yǔyán	n.	73
later	后来	hòulái	adv.	73
leisure	休闲	xiūxián	adj.	56
Li Bai, an ancient Chinese poet	李白	Lǐ Bái		104
life	生活	shēnghuó	n.	80
like that; in that way; then	那么	nàme	pron.	25
literature	文学	wénxué	n.	104
local specialty	特产	tèchǎn	n.	121
lovely, lovable	可爱	kě'ài	adj.	15
luggage	行李	xíngli	n.	121
major, subject	专业	zhuānyè	n.	183
many; a lot of	许多	xǔduō	adj.	25
maybe, perhaps	可能	kěnéng	adv.	183
meal	饭	fàn	n.	121
meat	肉	ròu	n.	49
medicine	药	yào	n.	63
method, way	方法	fāngfǎ	n.	73
microblog	微博	wēibó	n.	152
more and more	越来越	yuèláiyuè		73

英文	生字词	拼音	词性	页码
museum	博物馆	bówùguǎn	n.	25
name card; (business) card	名片	míngpiàn	n.	1
nationality	国籍	guójí	n.	176
net friend	网友	wǎngyǒu	n.	80
New York City	纽约	Niǔyuē	n.	97
news	消息	xiāoxi	n.	145
next one	下一个	xià yí gè	n.	87
not expect	没想到	méi xiǎngdào		159
office	办公室	bàngōngshì	n.	39
one time	一下	yíxià		63
online	在线	zàixiàn		145
only, just	只	zhǐ	adv.	176
or	或者	huòzhě	conj.	39
other	别的	biéde	pron.	8
outside, outdoor	外面	wàimiàn	n.	169
panda	熊猫	xióngmāo	n.	56
park	公园	gōngyuán	n.	25
parking lot	停车场	tíngchēchǎng	n.	128
passerby	路人	lùrén	n.	121
passport	护照	hùzhào	n.	121
pet	宠物	chǒngwù	n.	63
photograph, picture	照片	zhàopiàn	n.	15
pocket money	零用钱	língyòngqián	n.	169
poet	诗人	Shīrén	n.	104
police bureau; police station; police department	警察局	jǐngchájú	n.	39
post office	邮局	yóujú	n.	32
postage stamp	邮票	yóupiào	n.	32
practice; to practise	练习	liànxí	n./v.	73
price	价钱	jiàqián	n.	135
Putonghua; Mandarin Chinese	普通话	Pǔtōnghuà	n.	15
Qu Yuan, an ancient Chinese poet	屈原	Qū Yuán		104

英文	生字词	拼音	词性	页码
question, problem	问题	wèntí	n.	128
quiet	安静	ānjìng	adj.	183
recently, lately	最近	zuìjìn	adv.	145
refrigerator	冰箱	bīngxiāng	n.	135
restaurant	餐厅	cāntīng	n.	49
right	对	duì	adj.	73
right away	马上	mǎshàng	adv.	73
road, path, way	路	lù	n.	1
satisfied, pleased	满意	mǎnyì	adj.	8
school begins	开学	kāi xué		183
sea	海	hǎi	n.	56
seem; as if	好像	hǎoxiàng	adv.	169
senior	老人	lǎorén	n.	49
sentence	句	jù	n.	87
seperately	分别	fēnbié	adv.	87
service	服务	fúwù	n.	159
shoes	鞋	xié	n.	111
shop, store	商店	shāngdiàn	n.	135
shopping mall	商场	shāngchǎng	n.	111
short	短	duǎn	adj.	111
should; ought to	应该	yīnggāi	v.	63
skating; to skate	滑冰	huá bīng	n./v.	56
skirt	裙子	qúnzi	n.	111
slow	慢	màn	adj.	152
soup	汤	tāng	n.	49
south; in the south of China	南方	nánfāng	n.	183
speed	速度	sùdù	n.	152
sportswear	运动服	yùndòngfú	n.	97
star	明星	míngxīng	n.	97
straight for ward; all through	一直	yìzhí	adv.	25
subway, underground, tube	地铁	dìtiě	n.	39
such as	比如	bǐrú	v.	87

英文	生字词	拼音	词性	页码
suitable, appropriate	合适	héshì	adj.	15
summer holiday	暑假	shǔjià	n.	56
sun	太阳	tàiyáng	n.	121
sweater	毛衣	máoyī	n.	111
swimming pool	游泳池	yóuyǒngchí	n.	32
Tai Chi, shadow boxing	太极拳	tàijíquán	n.	159
team	队	duì	n.	97
temperature	体温	tǐwēn	n.	63
ten thousand	万	wàn	num.	152
that very day	当天	dàngtiān		97
the Internet	网络	wǎngluò	n.	80
the tradional Chinese calendar	农历	nónglì	n.	104
the whole family	全家	quán jiā		128
then and only then	才	cái	adv.	80
these	这些	zhèxiē	pron.	1
thin, slim	瘦	shòu	adj.	49
thirsty	渴	kě	adj.	49
thousand	千	qiān	num.	104
Tian'anmen Square	天安门广场	Tiān'ānmén Guǎngchǎng	n.	25
to answer; answer	回答	huídá	v./n.	87
to be away from; to leave; to part from	离	lí	v.	32
to be born	出生	chūshēng	v.	8
to be free	免费	miǎnfèi	v.	32
to borrow	借	jiè	v.	169
to bring, to take	带	dài	v.	
to change	变	biàn	v.	183
to change, to exchange	换	huàn	v.	128
to check	量	liáng	v.	63
to check; to look up	查看	chákàn	v.	80
to come across	遇到	yùdào	v.	97

英文	生字词	拼音	词性	页码
to come from	来自	láizì	v.	1
to decide	决定	juédìng	v.	183
to design; design	设计	shèjì	v./n.	145
to download; download	下载	xiàzài	v./n.	145
to draw, to paint	画	huà	v.	159
to exchange	交流	jiāoliú	v.	1
to exercise	练习	liànxí	v.	159
to exhibit	展览	zhǎnlǎn	v.	145
to finish; to be over	结束	jiéshù	v.	176
to forget	忘	wàng	v.	73
to get in touch with; to contact	联系	liánxì	v.	1
to get, to obtain	得到	dédào	v.	176
to go for a walk or stroll	散步	sànbù	v.	32
to go on; to continue	继续	jìxù	v.	87
to graduate; graduation	毕业	bìyè	v./n.	15
to have a discount	打折	dǎ zhé	v.	135
to have a sleep	睡觉	shuìjiào	v.	49
to interview	采访	cǎifǎng	v.	159
to join	参加	cānjiā	v.	73
to know	了解	liǎojiě	v.	135
to know, to understand	懂	dǒng	v.	73
to let	让	ràng	v.	80
to like, to love	爱	ài	v.	49
to live, to stay	住	zhù	v.	25
to make money; to make a profit	赚钱	zhuàn qián	v.	8
to name	起（名字）	qǐ(míngzi)	v.	159
to need	需要	xūyào	v.	176
to order dishes	点菜	diǎn cài	v.	121
to pay	付钱	fù qián	v.	121
to pick up	接	jiē	v.	97
to produce	出	chū	v.	183
to receive, to accept	收到	shōudào	v.	32

英文	生字词	拼音	词性	页码
to remember	记	jì	v.	73
to remember	纪念	jìniàn	v.	104
to remember, to recollect	想起来	xiǎng qǐlái	v.	169
to reply (letter, mail, phone call, etc.)	回（信）	huí (xìn)	v.	145
to return	还	huán	v.	169
to return to sb's mother country	回国	huí guó		128
to sell	卖	mài	v.	135
to send	送	sòng	v.	135
to send, to post	寄	jì	v.	32
to smile, to laugh	笑	xiào	v.	15
to solve	解决	jiějué	v.	128
to spend	花	huā	v.	73
to stop; to stop over	停	tíng	v.	25
to succeed	成功	chénggōng	v.	159
to take (a picture, photograph)	拍	pāi	v.	15
to talk	谈谈	tántan	v.	183
to try, to test	试试	shìshi	v.	8
to update, to renew	更新	gēngxīn	v.	152
to upload	上传	shàngchuán	v.	183
to visit	参观	cānguān	v.	56
to wear	穿	chuān	v.	63
topic, subject (of a talk or conversation)	话题	huàtí	n.	1
tour guide	导游	dǎoyóu	n.	8
toward, to	向	xiàng	prep.	152
traditional Chinese painting	国画	guóhuà	n.	145
traffic, transportation	交通	jiāotōng	n.	39
trousers	裤子	kùzi	n.	111
T-shirt	T恤	T-xù	n.	111
TV station	电视台	diànshìtái	n.	159
umbrella	雨伞	yǔsǎn	n.	111